ONLY A GREAT RAIN

ONLY A GREAT RAIN

A Guide to Chinese Buddhist Meditation

by Master Hsing Yun
translated by Tom Graham

Introduction by John McRae

WISDOM PUBLICATIONS • BOSTON

Wisdom Publications
199 Elm Street
Somerville MA 02144 USA

Library of Congress Cataloging-in-Publication Data
Hsing-Yün-ta-shih.
      Only a great rain : a guide to Chinese Buddhist meditation / by
   Master Hsing Yun ; translated by Tom Graham ; introduction by
   John McRae.
         p.   cm.
      Includes index.
      ISBN 0-86171-148-3 (pbk. : alk. paper)
   1. Meditation—Buddhism. 2. Buddhism—China—Doctrine.
   I. Graham, Tom (Thomas Boyd), 1951–   . II. Title. III. Title:
   Guide to Chinese Buddhist meditation.
   BQ5612.H75   1999
   294.3'4435—dc21   99-19502

ISBN 0-86171-148-3

04 03 02 01 00
 6   5   4   3   2

Cover by: Gopa & the Bear
Interior by: Gopa Design
cover image © 1998 PhotoDisc, Inc.

Printed in the United States of America

The billowing dust of the world
fills the sky and covers the sun.
Only a great rain can clear it.
In this way too, samādhi
stills the scattered mind
while contemplation clears the air.

—from the *Great Treatise on the Perfection of Wisdom*

CONTENTS

TRANSLATOR'S PREFACE

THE ESSAYS THAT MAKE UP this short volume give a clear and comprehensive view of Chinese Buddhist meditation techniques. Master Hsing Yun explains how to sit, when to sit, and what to do while meditating. The reader is presented with concise instructions on breathing, visualization, and contemplation.

I chose to translate these essays because they are rooted firmly in both the Buddhist and the Chinese meditation traditions and because they will be useful both to beginning meditators and to those who are more experienced.

Master Hsing Yun stands squarely in the midst of a great tradition of Chinese Buddhist writers whose styles are exemplified by brevity, precision, and clarity. I hope that I have been able to capture in these English translations some sense of the spirited force and certainty that pervades the original Chinese. I also hope that this small volume will help to further the world's appreciation of the depth and beauty of the Chinese Buddhist tradition.

I wish to thank Master Hsing Yun for providing me with the opportunity to translate these essays. I also want to thank Venerable Yi Jih for the many hours she has spent teaching me both Buddhism and Chinese. Thanks also to Jeff Jenkins, who is an unparalleled Buddhist conversationalist.

May any and all merit that may accrue from these translations be shared by sentient beings everywhere.

Tom Graham

INTRODUCTION

THE UNSPOKEN ASSUMPTIONS
OF BUDDHIST MEDITATION

BUDDHIST MEDITATION is the most important enterprise of our human existence. To be sure, eating, breathing, and sleeping are human needs of far more pressing urgency, but we should not mistake the mere basics of our animal realities for the common denominator of our being. To understand who we are and who we are not, to see clearly both the possibilities and liabilities of our current situations, to ground our actions in an enlightened concern for other living beings, to work ceaselessly for both our own betterment and that of all others—all these goals and more are encompassed within the realm of Buddhist meditation. Meditation is the very heart of Buddhism itself, the primary message of Śākyamuni Buddha to the world.

This all-important heart of Buddhism, its doctrine of self-cultivation and enlightenment, is based on two largely unspoken assumptions. The first of these is that if you truly understand something, you will be free of its influence. This inextricable link between wisdom and liberation is rarely discussed, but virtually always assumed, in Buddhist writings. Why is it that wisdom should bring liberation? At the moment, I cannot think of anywhere within Buddhist scriptures where this question is raised; no doubt, my own learning is incomplete. Of course, the sort of understanding indicated here is not the discursive sort of book-learning to which I've just alluded, the kind that we cultivate in the classroom, nor even the intuitive "street smarts" we may gain from a life-time of human experience. The type of understanding to which I am referring here is beyond the ordinary sorts of comparison and categorization that we do in most of our mental activity, beyond any kind of sensory or extra-sensory perception. In Buddhism, this kind of non-discriminative understanding is generally referred to as *prajñā*. Those who have experienced undiluted moments of prajñā wisdom directed at the fundamental nature of our existence are thought to have achieved total transformation in their indi-vidual states of being, which render them morally perfected beings who have transcended all suffering. Simply put, such an experience of prajñā wisdom into the basic realities of the human condition constitutes enlightenment, which is thought of as carrying with it total liberation from all the problems of the human condition.

The second assumption is that prajñā is an innate capac-ity of the mind, so that if we merely point the mind at an object or topic, the mind's innate wisdom will be able to understand that object. Naturally, to merely point the mind at an object is easier said than done, but when this ability is achieved it allows one to focus the innate power of the mind, in a searchlight fashion, on any particular problem or issue one may choose. This process of focusing the mind on par-ticular issues is often referred to as *vipaśyanā* in Buddhist texts, a term rendered variously as "contemplation," "dis-cernment," or "insight meditation" in English. This term actually refers to an entire host of meditation exercises by which one may direct the mind's innate capacity of prajñā at different topics, so as to understand their true nature. The goal is to gain what is referred to simply as "clear comprehension" of, or "insight" into, the given topic, terms which mean merely that one understands the topic just the way it is, with no error or subjective distortion. As the reader will see below, the methods and topics of vipaśyanā or insight meditation are discussed in great detail in Buddhist writings. However, the basic assumption that the mind has the innate capacity of prajñā is rarely, if ever, discussed.

Based on these assumptions, the manifold tradition of Buddhist meditation practice provides a wide range of different techniques for persons of various dispositions and capabilities, so that each of us may work our own individual way toward the achievement of insight. Since the basic tendency of virtually all of us is to be hyperactive mentally, many of these techniques are presented as aids to achieving mental concentration. In contrast to vipaśyanā or insight meditation, such *śamatha* or "concentration" techniques are designed to train the mind to focus on a given object attentively, continuously, and without any distraction whatsoever. Such mental strength-building, if you will, is meant to overcome a wealth of ordinary human disabilities: For those inclined to greed, there are meditation exercises on the impurity of the human body; for those inclined to anger, there are techniques for the generation of compassion toward other beings; and for those inclined to ignorance, there are guided reflections on the myriad components of our experienced reality and their interaction. Naturally, some of these exercises blend subtly from concentration to insight, and any individual set of exercises can have multiple benefits. But the requirements and techniques of Buddhist meditation are far more specific, more elaborate, and more demanding than most readers would imagine. Buddhist meditation is a tradition of spiritual craftsmanship unparalleled in other cultural realms.

Only a Great Rain describes Buddhist meditation from the perspective of the Chinese Mahāyāna Buddhist tradition, through the eyes of one of its greatest living representatives, Master Hsing Yun of Fo Guang Shan. This is therefore a book with several levels of authority. First, Hsing Yun is the product of the Chinese tradition of Mahāyāna Buddhism, whose training in some of the most important monastic centers during the tumultuous middle decades of this century instilled in him a grasp of the tradition that is both profound and comprehensive. Second, Hsing Yun is the founder and spiritual leader of the largest Buddhist monastic organization in Taiwan today, and certainly one of the largest networks of ordained and lay Buddhist followers in the world. I am referring to the combination of the Fo Guang Shan system of temples and monastics and the Buddha's Light International Association of lay believers, with their various temples and branches on six continents. Third, through his many years of experience both as a Buddhist seeker himself and as the teacher of literally tens or hundreds of thousands, if not millions, of other Buddhists, Hsing Yun has learned to present the hallowed teachings of Śākyamuni Buddha in a clear and concise manner true to the Chinese Mahāyāna tradition. In addition, he enriches his writings with anecdotes and examples that are especially pertinent to our lives in these last days of the twentieth century.

In order to contextualize Master Hsing Yun's lucid explanation of Buddhist meditation in the pages that follow, let me briefly describe who Hsing Yun is, what he has managed to achieve thus far in his life, and how he has absorbed and reformulated the teachings of Buddhist meditation for presentation to modern readers. I should point out that I have had occasion to meet with Hsing Yun several times over the past decade or so and have cooperated with his followers in the organization of several academic conferences. While I am not in any sense a personal disciple of his, nor a member of his following in any of its diverse organizational modes, I am nevertheless profoundly impressed by his personal charisma and the vast contributions he has made to Buddhism in the latter half of this century.

HSING YUN OF FO GUANG SHAN

Hsing Yun was born in Chiang-tu, Kiangsu Province, China, in 1927. At the age of twelve he became a novice monk under Venerable Master Chih-k'ai at Ch'i-hsia Shan, a famous monastery on the outskirts of Nanjing that has a long history of strength in the Chinese Mādhyamika and Vinaya traditions (that is, the doctrinal explication of śūnyatā, the fundamental emptiness of all things, and the monastic regulations, respectively). He was fully ordained in 1941, at the early age of fourteen; this timing was no doubt accelerated by the vicissitudes of the wartime years, since normally full ordination is not allowed until age eighteen. Hsing Yun underwent formal monastic training at Ch'i-hsia Shan, then continued his training at Chiao-shan Buddhist College. Chiao-shan was noted for its hall dedicated to the combined practice of Ch'an meditation and Pure Land devotions, which perhaps helped Hsing Yun develop the inclusive attitude toward Buddhism he exhibits in *Only a Great Rain.*

Several years ago I heard Master Hsing Yun tell the following story about his introduction to formal Buddhist training. Having proceeded to Ch'i-hsia Shan for ordination, he and the other trainees had to work their way through a number of stations, where they registered and fulfilled various administrative procedures. I imagine the setting to be the monastic equivalent of being inducted into the army, with different officers waiting behind a succession of desks— in either case there was an entirely new protocol and hierarchy to be comprehended, and a number of different senior instructors or officers to be satisfied. At one of these registration stations Hsing Yun was asked by the senior monk in charge whether he had decided to take full ordination as a Buddhist monk out of his own initiative, or because he had been instructed to do so by his teacher. Realizing that Buddhist spiritual training had to be undertaken as the consequence of one's own intention to achieve perfect enlightenment for all living beings (*bodhicitta,* or the "bodhi mind"), Hsing Yun answered that he had come out of his own initiative. To his great shock, the senior monk then boxed him sharply about the ears and berated him loudly for lacking proper respect for his teacher. Duly chastened by this surprising and altogether unwelcome response, when the monk at the very next table asked him exactly the same question, the young Hsing Yun knew exactly how to reply: that he had come out of respect for his teacher's command. Imagine his surprise when, once again, he was slapped and berated, even more loudly than before, for lacking any spiritual initiative of his own!

Hsing Yun's response seems eminently reasonable in hindsight, although it must have taken considerable emotional and spiritual energy to maintain: he did not utter another word to anyone for the next year and a half!

Presumably, if no answer is correct, it is better not to say anything. And in an archaic, even feudal, monastic environment, it is perhaps understandable that "teaching" might be reduced to the inculcation of hierarchical subservience, that "monastic discipline" might be reduced to petty oppression. It is a mark of his own willingness to modify and adapt the Buddhist tradition to fit the needs of the contemporary era that Master Hsing Yun has declared the style of training just described entirely out of date and inappropriate for his own monastic training centers in Taiwan. One additional comment: In one of the movies made recently in Taiwan depicting the life of Bodhidharma, the founder of the Chinese Ch'an or "Zen" School, the same events are used to provide descriptive color to the life of the ancient patriarch. Actually, I don't know who modeled what on whom!

By his early twenties Hsing Yun was already designated abbot of a temple in Nanjing, and he also served as the principal of a public school and editor of a monthly journal. All of these early appointments represent signs of both the chaotic times in which he was living and his extraordinary leadership potential. In 1949 he moved to Taiwan, along with many other prominent Buddhist leaders who have subsequently contributed to the thorough revitalization of the religion there in the past several decades. His activities in Taiwan are breathtaking in their energy and scope: In addition to serving as editor of several different weekly and monthly publications, in 1952 he established a temple in the city of I-lan (about an hour's drive from Taipei), where he formed associations for the practice of the recitation of the name of the Buddha Amitābha and for disseminating Buddhism. He also established a Buddhist Sunday school and kindergarten and began disseminating Buddhism via radio around this time. Hsing Yun's earliest disciples date from the time of his preaching at the temple in I-lan during the years 1952–62. The associations he established during the same period represent the earliest phases of what would eventually grow to become some of Taiwan's—and the world's—most sizeable and energetic Buddhist organizations.

In 1955 Hsing Yun established his first temple in the city of Kaohsiung, near the southern tip of the island of Taiwan, and he followed this soon thereafter with an organization in Taipei for the publication of Buddhist books and recordings. (This was the forerunner of Fo Guang Publishers.) In 1962 he established a Buddhist college in Kaohsiung, and in 1967 he established Fo Guang Shan there. Construction at this temple continued over the ensuing three decades. The Buddha's Light International Association (BLIA) was established in 1990, and in 1992 the organization was made international with the inauguration of its world headquarters at Hsi Lai Temple in Hacienda Heights, California.

In addition to fifty-two temples in Taiwan, the Fo Guang Shan organization now includes temples in North and South America, Australia, Europe, Africa, and Asia. There are sixteen different Buddhist training colleges, and a research center for the study of Indian culture at Chinese Culture University in Taiwan. In addition, there have now been established two comprehensive institutions of higher learning: Fo Guang University in I-lan, Taiwan, and Hsi Lai University in Rosemead, California. In 1957 Fo Guang Publishers was established, which makes available a wide variety of religious and scholarly writings on Buddhism. Begun in 1977, an editorial committee working under Hsing Yun's leadership has produced an eight-volume encyclopedia of Buddhism (also available in CD ROM format) and new editions of three categories of Buddhist scripture (the

Āgamas or earliest Buddhist writings, the scriptures of Ch'an or Zen Buddhism, and the "perfection of wisdom" literature), with a fourth category (a Pure Land collection) now in progress.

Although it is difficult to keep track of everything that Master Hsing Yun has achieved, the latest enumeration of all the accomplishments of the greater Fo Guang Shan organization includes the following: 170 temples and over a hundred chapters of the Buddha's Light International Association around the world, four public universities, sixteen Buddhist colleges, twenty libraries, two publishing houses, nine art galleries, a free mobile health clinic, a television station, and one thousand two hundred nuns and two hundred monks. I have often heard it said that were Fo Guang Shan a commercial enterprise it would exceed all other Taiwanese corporations in the size of its holdings and extent of its activities.

At age seventy-one Hsing Yun has long since ceded active administrative supervision to his many disciples. (He retired as abbot of Fo Guang Shan in 1985.) Indeed, none of his work as an organization builder and administrator would have been possible were he not an effective and inspiring teacher, lecturer, and writer. He has written many books in addition to the present volume, and some of his writings and sermons are already available in English. Building on the literary achievements of Venerable Yin-shun, the grand patriarch of Buddhism in Taiwan, and the religious inspiration of Master T'ai Hsu, Hsing Yun has worked to define a humanistic Buddhism, the creation of a pure land here on earth.

BUDDHIST MEDITATION
IN THE CHINESE MAHĀYĀNA TRADITION

In the very middle of *Only a Great Rain* the author does a remarkable thing that reveals a crucially important feature of Chinese Mahāyāna Buddhism: he includes brief discussions of meditation practice in the Hua-yen, T'ien-t'ai, Pure Land, and Ch'an (or Zen) schools. (See chapter 2, "Ceasing and Contemplating.") In a way that is entirely unique for books on Buddhist meditation in English, this provides the reader with information that would otherwise be very difficult to find. But, more importantly, it indicates the extent to which Hsing Yun represents the whole of the Chinese Buddhist tradition and the extent to which that tradition transcends sectarian differences.

Although Chinese Buddhism is usually described in terms of its eight most important "schools," these are neither sectarian entities nor denominations, neither independent churches nor separate institutional organizations. Rather, "schools" in Chinese Buddhism are traditions of training and practice, legacies of religious style that are adopted and mixed to suit the tastes of the individual practitioner. I know that this definition must seem rather amorphous, but understanding the elusive identity of Chinese Buddhist schools is the first step in understanding the true nature of Chinese Buddhism.

Chinese Buddhist schools are fundamentally different from the schools of Japanese Buddhism, for example, which for unique historical reasons constitute hierarchically organized institutions with head and branch temples, specific doctrinal creeds and orthopraxies, and lists of member families. To put it another way, every Japanese temple belongs to an administrative institution called such-and-such a "school," which specifies acceptable doctrine and religious practice, and according to which the priests of the school are ordained and trained. And, on the other side of the coin, virtually every Japanese family is registered with a particular local temple, to which family members turn for funerals, memorial services, and other religious observations. (This system was established in the seventeenth century and has long since been breaking down in the face of social and religious change. These days many Japanese families know to which temple their family belongs back in its native home, usually far from their present places of residence in Tokyo or some other city, but they often do not know to which Buddhist school the temple belongs to.) Since Japanese Buddhist scholars have been so influential in developing our contemporary understanding of East Asian Buddhism, we have unconsciously adopted their quite understandable misconception that Chinese Buddhist schools are merely the continental counterparts to the Kegon (Hua-yen), Tendai (T'ien-t'ai), Pure Land (Jōdo in Japanese and Ching-t'u in Chinese), and Zen (Ch'an) schools of Japanese Buddhism.

Thus Japanese Zen masters teaching in the United States are easily identifiable according to their sectarian backgrounds. Suzuki Rōshi, the beloved founder of the San Francisco Zen Center, for example, was from the Sōtō School. The much earlier Shaku Sōen, the first Japanese Zen priest to teach in the Western Hemisphere, was from the Rinzai School. Nominally, these identifications can be correlated with their Chinese antecedents, so that the Sōtō School is understood to have developed from the Chinese Ts'ao-tung School, and the Rinzai School developed from the Chinese Lin-chi School. However, Chinese Lin-chi Ch'an Buddhism lacks the institutional specificity of Japanese Rinzai, so that when Master Hsing Yun is identified as the forty-eighth patriarch of the Lin-chi tradition, he should not be thought of as the only individual in the world now authorized to use that title—there must be more than a few other members of the forty-eighth generation, not only in his own sub-lineage!

Chinese Buddhist schools have no institutional component whatsoever, and even though large temples are often referred to as such-and-such a "Ch'an monastery," they really do not belong to the Ch'an School. The position of abbot in such large "public" monasteries may be controlled by Ch'an monks, who also direct the functioning of the temple's meditation hall. However, in some cases the temple may be a "teaching" monastery, in which members of the T'ien-t'ai School will exercise similar control. Or, in a small number of cases the temple may have a historical specialization in the Vinaya tradition, in which case one of its principal activities will be the organization of large ordination ceremonies—to which aspirants from all the sub-traditions of Chinese Buddhism would be welcome. (The temple at which Hsing Yun was originally ordained was one such as this.) In none of these cases, though, are the religious activities of the temple in question limited to Ch'an meditation, or T'ien-t'ai meditation and study, let alone to specialization in the Vinaya. Quite the opposite! In different corners of the monastery at different times of the month and year there will be groups of monastics and lay people reciting the name of the Buddha Amitābha or chanting the *Lotus Sūtra*. Or, a gifted monk will offer lectures or sermons on the meaning of the *Flower Garland* or *Hua-yen Sūtra*, or Mādhyamika doctrine, or the Vinaya. In other words, such large "public" monasteries are comprehensive centers of Buddhist teaching and practice, and only rarely and in limited ways do they restrict themselves to the dissemination of the teachings of individual "schools."

The situation is now somewhat changed, of course, both on the Chinese mainland and in Taiwan. There is neither space nor need to discuss the former here, and about the latter I need only point out that the Fo Guang Shan organization has developed as a comprehensive set of institutions that encompass all of the Chinese Buddhist tradition. That is, in one institutional network Master Hsing Yun has worked to recreate the entire Chinese Buddhist tradition, in all its depth and breadth. Therefore, Hsing Yun has authority to describe the teachings and practices of all Chinese Buddhist schools equally, since he "belongs" to all of them to the extent that he is inclined to include them in his teachings. This is a thoroughly natural and authentic development.

This supra-sectarian perspective is in fact present on almost every page of *Only a Great Rain.* Consider the sūtras and treatises Master Hsing Yun cites: the Āgamas of early Buddhism; Abhidharma texts on early Buddhist philosophy; Mādhyamika and Yogācāra treatises of Mahāyāna philosophy; texts now recognized as having been authored in China such as the *Awakening of Faith;* and of course major Mahāyāna scriptures such as the *Lotus Sūtra* and *Mahāprajñāpāramitā (Great Perfection of Wisdom) Sūtra.* It is such a rich collection! Given the orientation of this volume toward the general reader, it will not be possible to locate all of the texts Hsing Yun cites within the evolution of Buddhist literature over the past two millennia or so—such a task would be a major undertaking even in a work of critical scholarship. The reader should also be aware that, just as this is not a work of critical scholarship but rather one of deeply informed Buddhist teaching, so is this a book based on the Chinese rather than the Indian tradition. In this case, the differences between the two need to be recognized only

briefly. For example, when Hsing Yun states authoritative-
ly that there are 250 *prātimokṣa* rules for monks and 348 for
nuns, this is indeed the case in China. The precise numbers
are somewhat different in the Theravāda tradition of South-
east Asia and the Tibetan Vajrayāna schools. In a slightly
different vein, the reader should be aware that Hsing Yun's
definitions of terms utilize both the style and the content of
Chinese Buddhist exegesis. See the explanation of "ceasing,"
for example, where the author and translator have both
worked to clarify the extent to which this important term
differs in nuance from its Sanskrit antecedent, śamatha or
"concentration meditation," as I have explained it above.

The reader may be surprised at the emphasis Hsing Yun
places on moral training as a necessary requirement of meditation practice, but in this regard he is echoing a theme that
reverberates throughout the Buddhist tradition. In Hsing
Yun's terms, this is a teaching of all the Buddhas, not only
Śākyamuni Buddha of our own time. Indeed, he locates the
very beginnings of Buddhist doctrine in the *Verse of the
Seven Buddhas,* which he cites early in his text:

> *Do no evil ever.*
> *Do good always.*
> *Purify your mind.*
> *These are the teachings of all buddhas.*

By introducing this verse in this way, Master Hsing Yun
indicates his identity within a timeless tradition of Mahāyāna Buddhism: The practice of meditation is but one part
of the entirety of the Buddhist spiritual path, which begins
with the motivation to become perfectly enlightened in
order to help liberate all sentient beings, not merely oneself,
from the bondage of suffering. I hope that you, the readers

of this book, will undertake the practice of Buddhist meditation with this lofty dedication and deep sense of personal discipline, or that you will, at the very least, undertake to appreciate the full dimensions of this most significant of all human enterprises.

John R. McRae
Indiana University

CHAPTER ONE

THE THREE
TRAININGS

*The three trainings are the
supreme dhāraṇī. They can
purify all karma of body,
speech, and mind, and they
are loved by all people.*

from the
Mahāsaṃnipāta Sūtra

MEDITATION SHOULD NOT BE VIEWED as an isolated
practice that can stand on its own. To be effective,
meditation must be practiced along with morality and wisdom. Without a firm moral foundation, meditation will
never produce the wonderful results it should. Without wisdom, even if one's meditation produces good results, one will
not be able to use them or understand them as one should.

Meditation properly is one part of complete Buddhist
practice. It is very important for Buddhists to meditate, but
if one does not also uphold the precepts of Buddhism while
working to increase one's wisdom, it will be unlikely that
one's meditation will produce good results.

In Buddhism, morality, meditation, and wisdom are called
the three trainings *(trīni śikṣāṇi)*. They are grouped together
because it is essential that all three be practiced at once.

A Collection of Terms Used in Translation says, "Stopping what is evil is called morality. Contemplating the breath in peaceful conditions is called meditation. Overcoming evil to understand the truth is called wisdom."

The three trainings are sometimes also called the "three trainings without outflow." *Outflow* means thought or behavior that leads to karmic entanglement. Outflows are imperfections that bind us to delusion. The fewer outflows we have, the less deluded we will be. One of the principal goals of Buddhist practice is to end all outflows. Outflows are caused by greed, anger, ignorance, or some combination of these. Since beginningless time for an untold number of incarnations all of us have allowed ourselves to be bound to delusion by our greed, anger, and ignorance.

Śākyamuni Buddha taught the three trainings to free us from delusion. Through morality we control our outflows, through meditation we learn to find peace, and through wisdom we learn how to use our gains in the most effective way possible. Generally speaking, meditation should be based on morality while wisdom should be based on meditation.

In Buddhist sūtras the three trainings are often described as the "triumphant" trainings or the "superior" trainings that overcome all delusion. They are described in this way because they have the great power to lead us to *nirvāṇa*. Diligent and sincere practice of the three trainings can only bring us the greatest merit. They are "superior" because they cannot lead to error. Eventually, they will lead to our "triumphant" liberation from delusion.

The *Sūtra of the Bodhisattva Stages* says that the first of the three trainings—morality—corresponds to the four *pāramitās* of generosity, morality, patience, and diligence. The sūtra says that the second of the three trainings—meditation—corresponds to the pāramitā of meditation, while the third of the three trainings—wisdom—corresponds to the pāramitā of wisdom.

The three trainings are fundamental to Buddhism. All Buddhist practice rests on them.

MORALITY

Control of the mind is the basis of morality.
Samādhi depends on morality and
wisdom depends on samādhi.
—from the *Śuraṅgama Sūtra*

The importance of morality

The Sanskrit word for morality is *śīla*, which means "precepts" or "obligations." The moral rules followed by Buddhist monks and nuns are called *prātimokṣa* in Sanskrit. Lay Buddhists naturally should be more concerned with śīla than with prātimokṣa, but it is helpful for all Buddhists to have some understanding of prātimokṣa as well.

Prātimokṣa means "deliverance" or "absolution." Prātimokṣa are the 250 rules that govern the lives of Buddhist monks or the 348 rules that govern the lives of Buddhist nuns.

The *Four Part Vinaya* says, "Prātimokṣa means restraint. If you correctly follow all of the rules of monastic behavior, including the rules of living with others, the rules of basic behavior, and other good dharmas, then you will achieve samādhi." *Samādhi* is a profound state of meditative concentration. This passage tells us that moral restraint is fundamental to higher practice. Without careful observance of moral rules, neither samādhi nor wisdom can ever be attained.

Śīla involves all areas of life. Śīla can mean "chastity," "restraint," or "good disposition." It can be understood as a kind of moral or behavioral "coolness" that feels very comfortable to the one who possesses it. It is important to understand that basic morality must be founded on restraint. Certainly, morality involves more than just restraint, but the foundation of morality primarily depends on a practitioner's willingness to refrain from immoral acts. The five basic precepts taught by Śākyamuni Buddha are phrased solely in the negative—each of them is something Buddhists should *not* do. Our willingness to refrain from evil is the beginning of our growth toward ultimate liberation. Without this willingness there can be little or no growth toward higher levels of consciousness.

The Buddha taught that if one's śīla, or moral nature, is not pure, one will not be able to achieve samādhi.

The *Great Treatise on the Perfection of Wisdom* says, "Śīla means basic goodness. To behave well while not shirking one's duties is called śīla. Whether you have accepted the precepts of Buddhism or not, if your behavior is good then this is called śīla."

The *Treatise on the Resources of the Bodhi Way* says that the concept of śīla includes all of the following ten items: habit, character, coolness or chastity, calmness, quietness, stopping of all outflows, gravity, purity, leadership, and praise. This list was carefully chosen. The first three items are concerned with the character or behavior of the practitioner. The last seven items are the results of having first established a proper moral foundation.

Master Tao-hsuan of the T'ang Dynasty subdivided the concept of moral restraint into four categories or steps to help us better understand what the Buddha has asked us to do. In his *Revision of the Four Part Vinaya*, he said that moral restraint consists of these four: the rules of Buddhism, the internalization of these rules, the behavior that results from these two, and the example one sets by these three.

1) The rules of Buddhism mean the precepts of Buddhism. The five basic precepts of Buddhism are: no killing, no stealing, no sexual misconduct, no lying, and no use of drugs or alcohol. Following these precepts is the first step in achieving moral purity.

2) Once one has learned to restrain oneself according to the precepts, one begins the process of internalizing them. As one comes to understand them more and live by them with greater faithfulness, the precepts of Buddhism will begin to transform one's character in a very profound way.

3) Once one has successfully internalized the precepts taught by the Buddha, one's behavior will naturally become very pure since it will be flowing entirely from pure sources.

4) Once one's behavior has become truly pure and undefiled, one will naturally begin to set an excellent example for others to follow. One's inherent kindness and decency will give hope to others as it persuades them by its goodness alone.

Master Tao-hsuan emphasized that, of the above four steps, internalizing the precepts is the most important. When we have deeply internalized the moral injunctions of the Buddha, we will have gone a very long way in our search to realize the truth. In the beginning, our faith tells us that this is so. In the end, our wisdom assures us that the Buddha did indeed lead us with exquisitely perfect teachings.

Buddhist sūtras are full of metaphors that are designed to help us understand the importance of moral restraint.

1) The sūtras say that moral restraint is like a good teacher because it shows us how to make quick progress in Buddhism. In the *Sūtra of Bequeathed Teachings*, the Buddha says, "After my *parinirvāṇa*, the prātimokṣa rules must be respected for they are like a light in the dark or like a treasure to a poor person. After my parinirvāṇa, they will be your master."

2) The sūtras say that moral restraint is like a clear path through the wilderness. If we stay on the trail, we will not get lost. If we decide to wander from the trail, then we probably will get lost and bring great harm to ourselves. It is important for Buddhists not to seek shortcuts or to believe that they know the way to liberation better than the Buddha does. Should we not trust him at least as much as we would a highway map or a road sign?

3) The sūtras say that moral restraint is like a walled well in a town. If our well is nearby, we will not have to travel far to get water. And if our well is protected by a wall, then even if we are besieged by enemies, we will still be assured of having a good source of water. Shortly before his death, the Buddha told his disciples:

Uphold the precepts, and do not allow yourselves to be deficient in any of them. If you can be wholly pure in upholding the precepts, you will achieve all good dharmas. If you are not pure, however, you will not successfully give rise to any good merit. Understand this: moral restraint is the primary source of all merit.
—from the *Sūtra of Bequeathed Teachings*

4) The sūtras say that moral restraint is like water that washes and cleanses us. As we go through the day, our bodies

become unctuous and dirty. If we do not have water to wash ourselves with, we soon become repugnant both to ourselves and to others. When we frequently restrain ourselves, it is as if we were frequently washing away the filth that inevitably adheres to beings in this realm.

5) The sūtras say that moral restraint is like a bright light. In the same way that ships are guided at night by the beacon of a lighthouse, so moral restraint can guide us safely past dangerous shoals. In the same way that a lantern can guide us on a dark trail at night, so moral restraint can guide us toward our indwelling buddha mind. The lamp of morality, once lighted, will quickly show us the purity that already lies within.

6) The sūtras say that moral restraint is beautiful in and of itself. Immoral people believe that beauty lies in rare and expensive things. One who practices morality quickly discovers, however, that the most beautiful things of all are virtue, goodness, and decency, and the natural kindness that flows easily from a moral nature awake to itself.

The different kinds of moral rules

In this section, I will briefly outline the most important moral rules observed by Buddhists. It is helpful for all Buddhists to have some familiarity with these rules. The Buddha intended that the rules for monastics and lay followers would form the foundation of their samādhi. Rules for monastics do not differ in kind from rules for lay followers —they are just stricter.

As we study these rules, it is helpful to remember that the Buddha made many very specific rules, especially for monastics. The specificity of his rules shows that he was very clear about the details of human behavior and of how very small things can cause enormous problems. Some of the rules dating from the Buddha's time no longer apply today—most of us have no need for an injunction against raising silk worms, for example. As we recognize that times have changed, however, we must also recognize that the spirit and purpose behind Śākyamuni Buddha's injunctions have not changed at all. None of us can claim to have followed his precepts if we have not long engaged in a close examination of our daily moral behavior.

1) General rules and particular rules

When buddhas first appear in this or any other world, their first disciples are generally very pure beings who are able to benefit from constant contact with a buddha. For this reason, the first moral injunctions of the seven buddhas of this world were stated simply and in general terms. In the beginning there was no need for detail in these matters. *The Verse of the Seven Buddhas* reveals the purity of those times in its simplicity. The verse says:

Do no evil ever.
Do good always.
Purify your mind.
These are the teachings of all buddhas.

The Verse of the Seven Buddhas expresses perfectly the general morality taught by Śākyamuni Buddha. It provides us with a core instruction that will serve us well in nearly all situations.

As the Buddha gradually gathered more disciples around him, it soon became clear that one general rule would not suffice for all of them. Buddha divided his followers into seven groups and made particular rules of behavior explicit for each of these groups. Some of the Buddha's particular rules apply to each of the seven groups, while some do not.

The seven groups are: *upāsaka* (male lay Buddhists), *upāsikā* (female lay Buddhists), *śrāmaṇeraka* (postulant monks), *śrāmaṇerikā* (postulant nuns), *śikṣamāṇa* (novice nuns), monks, and nuns. Each of these groups will be discussed in more detail below.

2) Restrictive rules and active rules

Restrictive rules are intended to prevent the creation of bad karma while active rules are intended to nurture meritorious behavior. The first line of *The Verse of the Seven Buddhas*—"Do no evil ever"—is a general example of a restrictive rule. The second line of the same verse—"Do good always"—is an example of an active rule or injunction.

3) Restrictions on acts that are essentially evil and restrictions on acts that often lead to evil

The Buddha said that killing, stealing, sexual misconduct, and lying are all acts that are essentially evil. These acts are recognized as evil in nearly all societies in the world. Drinking alcohol, on the other hand, is not essentially evil, since no one is directly harmed by the mere act of a person's drinking. The Buddha proscribed the use of alcoholic beverages, however, because they often lead to evil behavior. Alcohol and drugs cloud the mind and dim the light of reason. When people are inebriated, they all too often make bad decisions that can have serious consequences. No killing, no stealing, no sexual misconduct, and no lying are the first four of the five precepts of Buddhism. No use of drugs or alcohol is the fifth.

4) Rules for *śrāvakas* and *bodhisattvas*

Śrāvaka means one who has actually heard a buddha

speak. Needless to say, it is a wonderful thing to hear a buddha speak. However, the mere fact that one has heard a buddha speak does not mean that one has understood him perfectly. Śrāvakas are distinguished from bodhisattvas by their intentions; generally speaking, śrāvakas are principally concerned with their own enlightenment while bodhisattvas are concerned with the salvation of all sentient beings. For the most part, rules for śrāvakas are quite formal and specific. They can be found in the *Four Part Vinaya* and the *Vinaya in Ten Recitations.*

Rules for bodhisattvas are grouped under three basic categories: basic restrictions, basic good deeds, and basic beneficial deeds. The *Treatise on the Sūtra of Discrimination* says that the difference between śrāvaka and bodhisattva rules can be conceived of metaphorically as follows: the śrāvaka rules are like holding an arrangement of flowers on your knees—one false move and they will scatter. In contrast, the rules for bodhisattvas are like wearing flowers in your hair—you can dip your head and move without fear of dropping them.

5) Rules for lay Buddhists

Male lay Buddhists are called upāsaka while female lay Buddhists are called upāsikā. Lay followers should abide by the five precepts of Buddhism. Without this basic foundation, it is nearly impossible to progress in Buddhism. In addition to the five precepts, lay followers are encouraged to take an occasional monastic retreat during which they will follow many of the rules for monks or nuns for one day. During these retreats, retreatants may not wear make-up or perfume or listen to music, they may not sleep in a luxurious bed, they may not eat after noon, and they may not engage in any form of sexual activity. These restrictions plus the remaining basic precepts of not killing, stealing, lying, and taking intoxicants are called the eight precepts.

6) Rules for monastics

A) *Rules for postulant monks and nuns*. The process of becoming a fully ordained monk or nun first requires that the rules for postulants be observed. These rules are the ten precepts, which consist of the eight precepts discussed above with the addition of two more precepts: a stricter rule against eating after noon and a prohibition against the handling of money.

B) *Rules for śikṣamāṇa*. Śikṣamāṇa are novice nuns. Buddhist nuns are generally required to undergo a two-year waiting period prior to full ordination, though this waiting period often is shortened. The original purpose of this waiting period was to accustom novices to the rigors of monastic life and to make certain that they were not pregnant. During this period, novices must follow the six guidelines *(saddharma):* no sensual contact with others, no stealing, no killing any living creature, no lying whatsoever, no eating after noon, and no use of alcohol.

C) *Rules for fully ordained monastics*. These rules are extremely specific. There are 250 rules for monks and 348 for nuns. The following brief discussion of the kinds of transgressions monastics must guard against will help to explain the larger significance of all of the monastic rules.

i) *Pārājika*. Pārājika is a Sanskrit word meaning "defeated." It is used to denote an extremely serious offense that requires the expulsion of a monk or nun from the order. Examples of this kind of behavior are murder, serious theft, rape, or serious acts of lying or fraud.

ii) *Saṅgaveṣa*. This is a Sanskrit word meaning "remainder in the *saṅgha*." A monastic who commits an offense of this type is like a candle flame in the wind—his position in the monastery is extremely precarious. To prevent expulsion, he must repent and apologize before the entire monastery. There are thirteen kinds of behavior that are classified as saṅgaveṣa for monks. These include: intentional seminal emission, sexual touching, using sexual language when speaking to a woman, using false pretenses to touch a woman, acting as a match-maker, living in luxurious quarters, slander, libel, disobedience, encouraging disobedience, and vicious disobedience. For nuns, seventeen kinds of behavior are classified as saṅgaveṣa. They are roughly the same as the ones for monks.

III) *Aniyata.* Aniyata means "uncertain." This category covers offenses whose severity is not immediately apparent. In cases like this, other factors must be considered, including the offender's motives and the conditions under which he or she acted.

IV) *Pāyattika.* Pāyattika means "downfall." There are two basic kinds of pāyattika.

a) *propelled downfall.* Offenses of this sort generally involve a misuse of daily items. Having too many clothes, not lending things to others, or petty misuses of common things are examples of this. Offenders must publicly repent and publicly show the item or items they have misused.

b) *single downfall.* There are ninety offenses of this sort. All of them are relatively mild, though each must be exculpated by an apology and an act of repentance aimed at the one who was offended. Examples of this are misspeech or unintentional acts of rudeness.

v) *Pratideśanīya.* These are small offenses that can be corrected by apologizing and repenting.

vi) *Duṣkṛta.* These are small lapses in good behavior or thoughtless violations of the rules, such as dressing improperly or being ill-mannered.

vii) *Sapta adhikaraṇa śamathāḥ.* These are the seven methods used for ending disputes. Please consult chapter 52 of the *Madhyamāgama* if you want more detail on this subject.

This brief summary of Buddhist monastic and lay precepts was intended to help us understand the emphasis Buddha placed on moral behavior. Basic morality for all Buddhists should be conceived of as restraining ourselves from doing evil. Once we have learned to restrain ourselves, we will have begun to stop our outflows and thus our entanglement in *saṃsāra.* As this process of restraint becomes habitual, we will discover that we have been laying the foundation for samādhi and wisdom. The Buddha stressed morality for a very good reason: no one can realize higher levels of consciousness without it. The Buddha knew that human beings must first control their behavior before they can be expected to control their minds. That is why he taught the three trainings.

In the *Saṃyuktāgama,* Buddha says:

When I speak about the general principle of morality, listen carefully and think about what I am saying. This general principle can be understood by thinking as follows: If I knew that someone intended to kill me, I would not be happy. If this thought makes me unhappy, then I should realize that my intending to kill someone else would not make them happy. This realization should stop me from killing other sentient beings or from taking joy in the deaths of other sentient beings. In this same way, if someone's stealing from me makes me unhappy, then I should realize that my stealing from them will make them unhappy, and thus I should not steal. In this same way I should understand that, since I do not like others to take liberties with my wife, I should not take liberties with their wives. In this same way I should understand that, since I do not like being cheated by others, I should not cheat them. And since I do not like having poor relations with my friends or family, I should not cause discord in the relations between others. And since I do not like to be disparaged, I should not disparage or insult others. And since I do not like to be with those who engage in idle speech, I should not engage in idle speech myself. The above-mentioned ways of thinking are the general principles behind the precepts of no killing, no stealing, no sexual misconduct, no lying, no divisive speech, no duplicity, no harsh speech, and no idle speech. These are the precepts of saints.

The *Four Part Vinaya*, the *Mūlasarvāstivāda-vinaya-kṣudrakavastu*, the *Five Part Vinaya*, and the *Vinaya in Ten Recitations* all say that Buddhist morality in general has ten basic purposes:

1) To foster harmony among the saṅgha and lay followers alike.
2) To purify the saṅgha so that its members will be fit to lead lay followers.
3) To subdue stubborn and selfish tendencies among all Buddhists.
4) To provide a means of repentance to those who have committed transgressions and to give them an opportunity to find inner peace afterward.
5) To give all practitioners a chance to abide in the *Dharma* and make steady progress.

6) To help those who have no faith learn faith.

7) To help those who have faith increase their faith as well as their commitment to Buddhism.

8) To provide rules for speech and behavior so that all Buddhists will have the means to rid themselves of suffering.

9) To provide the means for Buddhists to achieve samādhi after they have rid themselves of suffering and to provide the means for them to prevent future suffering.

10) To give Buddhism a foundation so that it can exist for a long time.

Proper moral behavior can release us from the sufferings of this world as it provides the foundation for higher growth. This section has been somewhat detailed because morality is the essential foundation for samādhi. Without morality and restraint, the mind will surely entrap itself again behind the bars of saṃsāra. Without a strong moral foundation, progress in meditation is not possible.

Do no evil ever.
Do good always.
Purify your mind.
These are the teachings of all buddhas.

MEDITATION

All buddhas and all protectors of the true
Dharma are pure in body, speech, and mind.
As a result, they are pure in morality, samādhi,
and wisdom. By this they gain liberation and
perfect understanding.
　　　　　　—from the *Mahāsaṃnipāta Sūtra*

The meaning of samādhi

Samādhi is a Sanskrit word that means to concentrate. The word for samādhi in Chinese also carries the connotation to establish or make firm. Samādhi denotes a meditative state characterized by tranquil imperturbability. One who is in samādhi cannot be disturbed by external sensations. Samādhi is a nondual state of mind and one of the five attributes of the *dharmakāya*, a buddha's spiritual body. The wisdom of the *tathāgata* is founded on samādhi.

Meditators who know how to enter samādhi gain great powers. They are not easily distracted, and they are able to work with great energy and determination. In samādhi, the very wisdom and awareness of the tathāgata is discovered. The strength and wisdom that one gains from samādhi are two of the most important tools available to anyone who desires enlightenment.

Since the effects of samādhi are so wonderful, it has always been an important part of every Buddhist school. Meditation is not an exclusively Buddhist practice. In Śākyamuni Buddha's lifetime, many people in India knew how to meditate. Buddhist meditation techniques first began entering China toward the end of the second century of the Common Era. These techniques gradually intermingled with native Chinese techniques, producing a tradition of meditation that draws deeply on the wisdom of both cultures.

The T'ang Dynasty Zen master, Tsung-mi (780–841), said that there are five basic kinds of samādhi.

1) Ordinary samādhi. This kind of samādhi is devoid of religious or philosophical wisdom. Its sole value lies in its ability to help cure illness or strengthen the mind. Since people who practice this kind of samādhi are ignorant of the deeper levels of meditation, their practice can do nothing to free them from the cycle of birth and death.

2) Non-Buddhist samādhi. When non-Buddhists meditate, they may gain many rewards and many insights. However, since they do not realize the inherent emptiness of all phenomena, they will not reach the highest levels of understanding. Their practice may cause them to be reborn in heaven, but when their karma there is through, they will fall once again into the lower realms of existence.

3) *Hīnayāna* samādhi. Hīnayāna means "lesser vehicle." Hīnayāna samādhi is a term used to describe a practice of Buddhists who know how to help themselves, but are unable or unwilling to help others. This kind of samādhi is better than ordinary samādhi or the samādhi of non-Buddhists since it is based on the teachings of the Buddha, but since it is fundamentally self-centered, it is not the highest samādhi.

4) *Mahāyāna* samādhi. Mahāyāna means "great vehicle." It is called the great vehicle because the Mahāyāna practitioner is concerned with the welfare of others as much as he is concerned with his own welfare. One who knows Mahāyāna samādhi knows very much indeed. He understands the nature of delusion, nonduality, emptiness, the need for compassion, and all of the other profound ideas

within Buddha's teaching. His samādhi benefits both himself and others at once. It is a very great state.

5) Supreme samādhi. This is the samādhi of the buddhas, and all of the buddhas in the universe know this samādhi. It is the purest and highest level of awareness possible.

If you want to accomplish anything in this world,
you must use all of your mind or you will not succeed.
How much more important then
is it to practice samādhi on
the profound path of Buddha?
    —from the *Great Treatise on the Perfection of Wisdom*

How to achieve samādhi

The best way to achieve samādhi is to learn it through the practice of sitting meditation. After one has practiced sitting meditation for a long enough time, one will find that one is able to enter samādhi when walking in the woods or beside a mountain stream or through a meadow. Soon after this state is achieved, one will find that one is able to enter samādhi even on a busy street in the middle of a noisy city. Samādhi states are frail in the beginning, but with practice they become very strong.

In the beginning, one should learn how to enter samādhi in a quiet room with few distractions. The lighting should be subdued, but the room should not be dark, as darkness may induce sleep. It is good to have an altar to the Buddha in your meditation room, and it is good to bow before the Buddha and light some incense before you begin meditating. Gather your thoughts as you light the incense and focus your attention on the Buddha. Your seat should not be in the wind or sun, and your meditation room should not be damp. The purpose of meditation is to raise your awareness, not to make you ill.

Loose, comfortable clothes should be worn for meditation, and the stomach should not be full of food. It is best to wait at least one hour after eating before beginning to meditate. To prevent drowsiness, one should not feel tired when sitting down to meditate.

In general meditation is concerned with three areas: the body, the breath, and the mind. By learning how to control and pacify these three areas of our being, we learn how to perceive the awesome beauty of the buddha who already dwells within.

> *The greatness of samādhi*
> *is like the greatness of a king*
> *because samādhi controls everything.*
> —from the *Mahāprajñāpāramitā Sūtra*

Control of the body

The seven aspects of the seated Vairocana Buddha are a basic foundation for Buddhist meditation. We will discuss these seven aspects below.

1) The lotus position. Generally speaking, the lotus position is the best position for sitting meditation. The full-lotus position is a cross-legged position in which the feet rest on top of the thighs, just above the knees. The half-lotus position is a cross-legged position in which only one foot rests on top of one thigh while the other foot rests below the other thigh. The full-lotus position is considered the best position for meditation because it stabilizes the body very effectively. If this position is uncomfortable, the

half-lotus position should be used. If this position also is too uncomfortable, it is fine to meditate while sitting on a chair or on a low stool designed for meditation. The most important thing about whichever position you choose is that your back be straight and not touching anything.

Chinese sources generally recognize two kinds of full-lotus position. The position in which the left foot is placed on the right thigh and then the right foot is placed on the left thigh is used to gain blessings and is called the "auspicious position." When the order of placement of the feet on the thighs is reversed, the position is used for subduing demons and is called the "demon subduing position."

2) Position of the hands. Once a sitting position has been adopted, the hands should rest comfortably in the lap with the back of one hand resting on the palm of the other. The tips of the thumbs should lightly touch each other. This position is very good for the circulation of energies within the system and it is called the *dharma-dhātu mudrā*.

3) Position of the back. Since the spine is the principal nervous center of the body where the energies of the extremities gather, it is important that the spine be straight while meditating. People who have weak backs or who are unused to sitting without support may need some time to become used to sitting in this way. Most people should be able to sit correctly without too much practice. The spine should be straight in meditation, but it should not be rigid, stiff, or unnaturally straight. Above all, one should feel relaxed and comfortable in one's meditation position. Before long, one should enjoy the physical act of sitting down to meditate.

4) Position of the shoulders and chest. The shoulders should be held back comfortably in a position that allows the chest to relax so that the breath can flow smoothly.
5) Position of the neck and head. The head and neck both should be held up straight. If the head tips too far forward, circulation through the neck will not be at its best. If viewed from the side, the ears should be aligned directly above the shoulders. This position allows the breath to travel smoothly through the nose into the lungs and it provides excellent circulation throughout the abdomen and thoracic cavity. Some attention should be paid to the muscles at the back of the neck. If these muscles are relaxed and well aligned, the entire back will generally fall into place quite easily.
6) Position of the mouth. The jaw and lips should be lightly closed. The tip of the tongue should be held gently behind the front of the upper teeth.
7) The eyes. Beginning meditators will generally do better if they keep their eyes open slightly and stare at something two or three feet away. This will help prevent drowsiness.

These seven points are basic to one's physical posture while meditating. Below I will mention eight more points that are also important for achieving a comfortable and effective meditation position.

1) Peace. One's seat and the room in which one meditates should be arranged in a way that is conducive to feelings of peace and comfort.
2) Not being constricted. Tight clothing, belts, watches, glasses, jewelry, or any other garment that constricts circulation should be loosened or removed before meditating.

3) The seat. If one is using the lotus or half-lotus position, one should sit on a comfortable cushion that will not slide around or easily change its shape. A good cushion should be wide enough to support the legs and knees and it should be about four fingers thick.

If this position is not comfortable, a low stool designed for meditation can be used, as can the edge of a chair or the edge of a hard bed. Posture is very important in meditation. Since people's bodies and habits vary so much, however, it is impossible to set only one or two rules for sitting. Again, comfort and a straight spine that does not touch anything are basic to all good meditation positions.

4) Covering the knees. Since one's circulation slows down during meditation, it is important that your knees are kept warm. If the weather is cool, they should be covered with a small blanket or cloth.

5) Purifying the breath. Repeat the following action three times: inhale through the nose and exhale through the mouth. As you exhale, imagine that you are exhaling toxins and defilements from your system. Both your inhalations and exhalations should be slow and thoughtful. If you do not feel relaxed after doing this exercise, repeat it.

6) Twist your body a few times in both directions and then sit quietly without moving anymore. If your position does not feel right, twist again and sit quietly again. It is very important to sit still while meditating. Occasional movements can be tolerated, but every meditator should strive to achieve long periods of time during which there is no movement of the body at all.

7) The face. As with all other parts of the body, the face should be relaxed. A very slight smile, if this feels natural, is a good facial expression for meditating. One's face should not be rigid or stern.

8) The back should not lean against anything. During meditation, energies within the system will naturally begin to withdraw into the spine and then rise within it. If the back is leaning against something, this natural flow will be blocked.

The three most basic things to remember about your meditation position are comfort, motionlessness, and a straight spine that is not leaning against anything. Meditation should be enjoyable and thus one should make oneself as comfortable as possible. Motionlessness during meditation helps one harness and elevate all of the energies present in one's system. A straight spine that is not leaning against anything creates the channel for those energies to rise toward higher centers.

Samādhi is like pure, clean water
for it can wash away all defilements.
—from the *Great Treatise on the Perfection of Wisdom*

Control of the breath

The basic purpose of breath control is to transform rough or heavy breathing into slower and more refined breathing. Once the body is motionless and the breath is controlled, the mind will naturally become calmer. When we speak of "controlling" the breath, it is important to remember that one controls it by observing it. If you try to force your breath to become calm, you will only cause problems. Simple observation of the breath is the best way to make it slow and calm. Chinese sources generally recognize four kinds of breathing.

1) Windy breathing. This kind of breathing makes sounds in the nostrils.
2) Uneven breathing. This kind of breathing is quiet, but it is uneven and sometimes it stops and starts.
3) Unrefined breathing. This kind of breathing is quiet and even, but it is not refined. It does not feel as comfortable as the fourth kind of breathing.
4) Right breathing. This kind of breathing is quiet, even, refined, and very peaceful and enjoyable. This kind of breathing brings great peace to the mind and heart.

This fourth kind of breathing is attained most quickly by simply observing the breath. If you try to force yourself to breathe or feel a certain way, you will almost certainly fail. The peace you create around yourself in meditation will continue to grow with practice. In time, you will find that you can achieve peace and stillness easily. When the breath and the body are peaceful, the mind has, as it were, a place from which it can successfully contemplate and comprehend itself. When the breath and the body are peaceful, the mind can enter samādhi.

The importance of breathing can be seen in the following passage from the *Six Wondrous Teachings,* a very influential book on meditation that records a talk given by the great monk Chih-i (538–597) at Wa-kuan Temple in present-day Jiangsu Province. The precise date of this talk is not known.

The "wondrous door of following" opens the way to the sixteen exceptional dharmas. The first of these dharmas is watching the inhalation of the breath. The second is watching the exhalation of the breath. The third is watching the length of the breath. The fourth is watching the breath fill the entire body. The fifth is eliminating all bodily movements.

The sixth is absorbing happiness into the mind. The seventh is absorbing joy into the mind. The eight is absorbing all mental activities into the mind. The ninth is creating happiness in the mind. The tenth is uniting all the activities of the mind. The eleventh is discovering liberation in the mind. The twelfth is contemplating impermanence. The thirteenth is contemplating the scattering of all things. The fourteenth is contemplating desirelessness. The fifteenth is contemplating extinction. The sixteenth is contemplating perfect non-attachment.

Control of the mind

The untrained mind has a mind of its own. Meditators often compare it to a drunken ape who careens through the forest without purpose, without understanding, and without the slightest bit of self-control. Our minds seem to belong to us, and yet, as soon as we sit down with the idea that we would like to take a closer look at their workings, we find that they do not obey us at all.

The *Yogācārabhūmi Śāstra* says that there are nine different levels of meditative equipoise or "mental abiding." We can begin to learn how to control our minds by studying these stages of equipoise and comparing them to our own meditation.

1) Interiorized abiding. This is the first stage. In this stage, one turns one's attention away from the outside and draws it completely within.
2) Level abiding. In the beginning of this stage, the mind is interiorized, but its awareness is discontinuous and random. First there is one kind of awareness, then another, and then another. The way to work with this kind of

mental state is simply to allow your thoughts to flow. Follow them from moment to moment without becoming attached to any of them. With practice, this sort of discontinuous consciousness gradually settles into a state of peaceful evenness wherein awareness is clear and level.

3) Peaceful abiding. This stage is characterized by a wonderful calmness and peace. The arrival of this stage is like the arrival of autumn weather in temperate climates. It does not come all at once. As late summer moves toward fall and winter, the gradual cooling of the earth is manifested in fits and starts. A mere day or two of cool temperatures in September will be followed by sets of three or four days of even cooler weather in October. By November there will be cold snaps, and in December warm weather will have become a memory. In this metaphor, the onset of peaceful abiding is like the onset of autumn and winter. First one recognizes a slight change, and then soon one becomes accustomed to it. When you recognize the onset of peaceful abiding in your meditation, take notice of its qualities and appreciate its deepening.

4) Near abiding. In this stage one is able to experience periods in one's meditation during which delusive thoughts do not arise. In this stage one also learns how to tell when delusive thoughts are going to arise before they arise. With this ability one is able to shield one's meditation from both outer and inner distractions.

5) Control. In this stage one deeply understands the merits of samādhi, and one fully comprehends that the ten aspects are the causes of all delusion. The ten aspects are form, sound, smell, taste, touch, greed, anger, ignorance, maleness, and femaleness. In this stage one has conquered one's mind and one is no longer a victim of its excitability.

6) Great peace. This stage is characterized by the profound

calmness that comes from completely understanding that greed, anger, and ignorance are the sources of all delusion.

7) Supreme peace. In this stage, delusive thoughts have no chance of arising. The mind is in a completely natural state and very free. Whatever comes into it comes into it, and whatever goes away from it goes away simply and without leaving any residue.

8) Single-pointedness. In this state the mind is gathered into a single point—it rests within itself and is complete within itself. There is nothing lacking, and no interruption of consciousness can occur. Some effort is required to reach this state.

9) Equanimity. This state arrives only after long practice. No effort is required to reach it. In this state the mind has fully entered samādhi. Goodness remains without effort, and evil stays away without trying to enter.

While observing the above stages, it is always a good idea to ask yourself where your mind is. The buddha mind is beyond locality, and, since the depths of your mind are the buddha mind, your mind is fundamentally beyond locality as well.

Our attachment to delusive thinking is what holds us in saṃsāra. This same attachment is what prevents us from achieving deep samādhi in meditation. The most fundamental delusion of the mind is its stubborn need to grasp onto things—onto ideas, concepts, desires, forms, emotions, people, etc. The mind is like a big hand that always wants to snatch at everything that comes near. Chinese Buddhists use this need of the mind to attach itself to something as a tool to free the mind.

The *Graduated Explication of the Perfection of Meditation* teaches us five methods to use this very tendency to grasp at things as a means of freeing ourselves from this tendency.

The purpose of these methods is to trap the mind's habitual grasping in something that will free it from delusion.

1) Attach the mind to the crown of the head.

   The Chinese word for attach as it is being used here is *hsi,* which means to "bind," "attach," or "fasten." This same word is also used in Chinese to denote being bound to saṃsāra or to one's karma. As used in these five practices, hsi could be rendered as "concentrate" in English, but an important distinction would be lost. One uses the very same grasping nature of the mind to do these exercises as one uses to form desires or fears or any of the other attachments that bind us to this world.

   The *Graduated Explication of the Perfection of Meditation* advises us to "attach the mind to the crown of the head" as a way of overcoming drowsiness and torpor. The mind can be lazy in its attachments—sleep, confusion, and the muddled emotions of groping ignorance are often as attractive to it as the bright colors and forms of clearly perceived desires. When we elevate our lower attachments to the top of the head, we go a long way toward overcoming what binds us to delusion.

   The *Graduated Explication of the Perfection of Meditation* warns that in some cases overuse of this technique can lead to physical problems associated with winds in the body or with a desire to fly. If this happens, this technique should be discontinued.

2) Attach the mind to the places where the hair meets the scalp. This is a very good place to center the attention. It is easy to feel, and most people have good results when they try this technique. This practice often can lead to a near-visionary comprehension of the human skeleton and the transience of the body. In some cases, overuse of this

technique may cause the eyes to stare upward and perceive
brightly colored clouds or abstract mosaics of color. These
shapes may lead the mind into seeing even more confusing forms, and eventually one may faint. For this reason,
it is important not to overdo this kind of meditation.

3) Attach the mind to the inner nostrils.

The nostrils are the doorways that allow air to pass in and
out of the body. If we direct our attention to the inner
nostrils our mind soon becomes lost in the coming and
going of the breath. Soon no thoughts will arise at all.
This technique is very good for helping us to realize the
impermanence of our bodies and of all things. It is also
one of the best techniques for calming the mind and leading it into samādhi.

4) Attach the mind to the navel.

The navel is the "ocean of the breath." It is a central
source of life-energy in the human body. Due to its
importance, this point is also called the "central palace"
in Chinese. When we attach the mind to the navel in
meditation, we cause blood and lymph to flow into the
center of the body. This flow has great healing benefits,
and many kinds of diseases can be cured by it. When
using this technique, one may also have a vision of the
thirty-six major parts of the body recognized in Buddhism. This vision may lead to very deep samādhi.
Women should be careful not to use this technique very
often since it may cause excessive menstrual bleeding.

5) Attach the mind to the earth.

When we focus the mind on the area beneath our meditation cushions, we bring great stability to our meditation.

Of these five methods, attaching the mind to the inner
nostrils, the navel, and the earth are the most stabilizing and

usually the most effective. A general principle that should be borne in mind whenever one is meditating is, if the body becomes extremely light and starts to feel as if it is floating upward, one should lower one's center of attention. If the body begins to feel very heavy as if it were sinking down, one should raise one's center of attention.

> *Disentangling oneself*
> *from desire and evil ways*
> *requires both vision and wisdom.*
> *Disentangling oneself from the world*
> *and discovering inner joy*
> *is the start of meditation.*
> —from the *Great Treatise on the Perfection of Wisdom*

Ending meditation

Just as the process of preparing to meditate is important, so too is the process of arising from meditation. If we just jump up from our seats and rush around without a proper transition, we may lose what we have gained during meditation and we may even cause ourselves to feel ill.

When we enter meditation, we move away from what is rough and forceful toward what is refined and gentle. When we end meditation, we move in the opposite direction—the calm, gentle world of the luminous inner mind slowly must give way to the requirements of physical movement, speech, and the thoughts that carry us through the day.

If we abruptly stand up after meditating and throw ourselves back into the world, we may cause ourselves to get a headache or to develop stiffness in the joints, or some other physical problem. Thoughtless transitions from meditation back to ordinary consciousness may also contribute to

emotional stress or irritability. For these reasons, it is important to pay attention to the following five points when arising from meditation.

1) Change your focus to new conditions.

   When you have decided that it is time to end your meditation, you should shift your attention away from the
   inner toward the outer. As your mind begins refocusing
   on external sensations, you should concentrate on the
   process of coming out of meditation.

2) Open your mouth and exhale a few times.

   As you do this, imagine that the last poisons in your body
   are being expelled. Feel how your whole body participates
   in the act of breathing.

3) Move your upper body.

   First gently move your upper body back and forth a few
   times while you are still sitting, then slowly twist and move
   the other parts of your body without straining. Gently
   massage your shoulders, arms, hands, neck, and head.

4) Move your legs.

   After you have done the above, gently begin to move and
   straighten your legs. They should gradually begin to feel
   limber and secure. If you move them too suddenly, they
   may begin to feel stiff and uncomfortable.

5) Massage your skin.

   Gently massage your skin until you feel a pleasant tingling.

6) Massage your eyes.

   Once your body and hands have begun to feel re-stim-
   ulated, gently massage your eyes until you feel normal
   circulation returning to them. When your eyes feel
   comfortable and ready, open them.

7) Expel heat.

   Meditation often causes the body temperature to rise—

some people even perspire when meditating. Upon arising from meditation, it is important to expel this heat or
allow it to settle down. The body can be quite sensitive
after meditation. Unusual sensations should be respected, and your system should be allowed to return naturally
to its customary homeostasis.

Upon arising from meditation it is sometimes helpful to
reflect on why we meditate. Meditation is a technique for
calming our delusive thoughts so that true wisdom can at last
be born. As we gradually see through our mind's delusions,
our understanding of enlightenment slowly increases. As our
understanding increases, our desire for enlightenment also
grows. This desire is not a saṃsāric desire for power or psychic
abilities. It is a desire to improve our wisdom and compassion.
It is a desire to be of greater benefit to other sentient beings.
It is a desire to become as benevolent as a buddha.

The wisdom that grows in us through our practice of
meditation must be applied to our lives in the real world.
Meditation that is not a source of practical and socially
beneficial wisdom is probably misdirected meditation. Hui-
neng, the sixth patriarch of Zen Buddhism, said:

> What is sitting meditation? To remove ourselves from all
> external distractions and quiet the mind is called "sitting."
> To observe the inner nature in perfect calmness is called
> "meditation."

Hui-neng also said:

> To remove oneself from all outer form is called
> "meditation" (dhyāna). To be perfectly interiorized
> and still is called "samādhi."

Meditation will not carry you to another world, but it will reveal the most profound and awesome dimensions of the world in which you already live. Calmly contemplating these dimensions and bringing them into the service of compassion and kindness is the right way to make rapid gains in meditation as well as in life.

> *In meditation we leave*
> *the fires of defilement*
> *for the coolness of clear samādhi.*
> *And this feels just like the joy*
> *of falling into cool, clear water*
> *after burning in the heat of the sun.*
> —from the *Great Treatise on the Perfection of Wisdom*

WISDOM

> *When the World-honored One*
> *established the Dharma,*
> *he made three basic points.*
> *The first is morality,*
> *the second is samādhi,*
> *and the third is wisdom.*
> —Master Tao-an

What is wisdom?

Wisdom in Sanskrit is *prajñā*. The word prajñā is often left untranslated both in English and Chinese because prajñā wisdom is very different from what too often passes for wisdom in this saṃsāric world. Prajñā wisdom is the highest sort of wisdom recognized in Buddhism and the highest of the six pāramitās. Glimpses of prajñā wisdom lead sentient beings toward enlightenment. Without prajñā wisdom, enlightenment would not be possible. The *Mahāprajñā-pāramitā Sūtra* says, "Prajñā is the mother of all buddhas."

Three ways of cultivating prajñā

Buddhists generally recognize three basic ways of achieving prajñā.

1) Wisdom achieved through listening

   If one has the good fortune of being around wise people who understand the Dharma, then one will have the opportunity to develop prajñā through listening to them. One may also develop one's wisdom by reading sūtras and Dharma literature or by watching Dharma videos and movies.

2) Wisdom achieved through thinking

   After hearing the Dharma, one must think about it or it will do no good. Wisdom is a trait or condition of the mind. If the mind is not used in the acquisition of wisdom, wisdom cannot be acquired. If one refuses to think about what one has heard, no learning will be possible. Through thinking it is possible to realize the truth of the Dharma very deeply. Everything starts in the mind. When the mind begins to train itself in the Dharma, nothing can obstruct it from rapid and joyful growth.

   The Buddha taught four necessary principles to help us discriminate between truth and falsity or between wisdom and ignorance. He said that our understanding should follow the Dharma and not people, that it should follow the spirit and not the letter of the Dharma, that it should follow the true meaning of the Dharma and not

interpretations of that meaning, and that it should follow our deep wisdom and not shallow knowledge.

3) Wisdom achieved through cultivation

Once we have developed our wisdom through listening
to the Dharma and reflecting upon its meaning, then we
must begin practicing what we have learned. The practice
of Buddhism is often called cultivation, since one cultivates wisdom and good behavior in much the same way
that a farmer cultivates his fields. The ground of interaction between our thought and behavior is the main field
whereupon cultivation occurs. One grows in Buddhism
through a continuous process of watching one's behavior
and adjusting it to accord more and more closely with
the wisdom of the buddha within. Eventually, this
process of continuous cultivation will produce direct
perception of nonduality and the emptiness of all phenomena. This is a very joyous state.

The *Mahāprajñāpāramitā Sūtra* gives some explanation of
wisdom when Subhūti addresses Śāriputra as follows:

Śāriputra, if a bodhisattva continues to study like this, then
he will gradually draw closer to the perfect knowledge *(sar-
vajña)* of a buddha, and he will gradually become pure in
body, mind, and perception. When he is pure in body, mind,
and perception, then the bodhisattva no longer will give rise
to defilements, to anger, to ignorance, to pride, to greed, or
to mistaken views. When a bodhisattva no longer gives rise to
any of the above defilements, then he will no longer become
a body in a woman's womb, but instead he will achieve the
transformation body and move only from one buddha realm
to another, and he will help all sentient beings achieve the
purity of the buddha realm. Eventually, he will achieve *anut-
tara-saṃyak-saṃbodhi* and be one with all buddhas.

Our understanding of wisdom grows with our wisdom. Today wisdom seems to be one thing, tomorrow it will seem to be something even deeper and greater. As our capacity to understand the depth of the Dharma increases, our appreciation of what the Dharma teaches also increases. Throughout this growth process, it is imperative that the practitioner remember that any morality, any samādhi, or any wisdom that does not compassionately benefit all sentient beings can only be an imitation of the real thing.

The Buddha stressed the three trainings to help us avoid the imbalances inherent in cultivating only morality, only meditation, or only wisdom. It is important to understand this point. For the most part, most people are accustomed to holding fast to only one religious idea at a time—their religion is essentially based on faith, on belief, or on morality. The Buddha taught the three trainings to help us overcome this tendency to make our spiritual lives one-dimensional. Wisdom is often called the highest virtue in Buddhism because it is only wisdom that can understand the importance of practicing all of the three trainings at once.

The *Yogācārabhūmi Śāstra* says:

When one practices the three trainings, what stages of growth does one experience? First one becomes pure and good through the practice of morality, and this leads to an ending of anxiety. After ending anxiety, one begins to experience peaceful joy. With the onset of peaceful joy, one begins to experience proper samādhi. With proper samādhi, one begins to gain true knowledge and true insight, and these lead to a sense of revulsion for that which is false or evil. This revulsion helps one disentangle oneself from defilement, and this disentangling leads to liberation. Liberation eventually leads to perfect fulfillment in nirvāṇa.

This is the way one's growth proceeds: first one cultivates purity and morality, and gradually these lead to nirvāṇa.

In the *Mahāparinirvāṇa Sūtra*, Śākyamuni Buddha explains the importance of the three trainings very well:

Simhanāda Bodhisattva asked the Buddha, "World-honored One, what does it mean to cultivate morality, and what does it mean to cultivate samādhi, and what does it mean to cultivate wisdom?"

The Buddha said, "Good monks, if a person accepts the precepts only for the purpose of gaining heavenly pleasures for himself and not for the purpose of saving all sentient beings, then he is not upholding the supreme Dharma. If he acts only for his own benefit, or out of fear of falling into the lower realms of existence, or to make his life proceed pleasantly and smoothly, or because he fears the ordinary laws of the land or bringing harm to his reputation, then he is merely acting out of the immediate concerns of his life in this world. This kind of upholding of the precepts is not true cultivation of the precepts.

"Good monks, what is true cultivation of the precepts? If you cultivate the precepts for the purpose of saving all sentient beings and protecting the true Dharma, and if you save those who have not been saved, and if you liberate those who have not been liberated, and if you lead those who have not known nirvāṇa into nirvāṇa, and if, when you do these things, you do not notice the precepts or the form of the precepts, or that you are upholding the precepts, and if you take no notice of potential rewards and do not become seduced by lower forces—this, good monks, is what is called cultivating the precepts.

"And what is cultivation of samādhi? If a person cultivates

samādhi for the purpose of achieving his own liberation or his own benefit and not for the good of all sentient beings or for the protection of the Dharma, then he is not truly cultivating samādhi. If he is doing it out of greed, or lust, or attachment to food, or any other transgression of this sort, then he is not truly cultivating samādhi. The nine orifices of both the male and female body are not clean. To cultivate samādhi for the purpose of fighting and killing is not to cultivate true samādhi.

"Good monks, what is true cultivation of samādhi? If samādhi is cultivated for the good of all sentient beings, and if equanimity is attained among sentient beings for the purpose of helping them attain the Dharma beyond regression and for the purpose of helping them attain the saintly mind, and for the purpose of helping them attain the Mahāyāna way, and for the purpose of protecting the supreme Dharma, and for the purpose of helping sentient beings attain the *bodhi* mind without regression, and for the purpose of helping sentient beings attain *śūraṅgama* samādhi and diamond samādhi, and for the purpose of helping sentient beings attain the dhāraṇī and the four boundless states of mind, and for the purpose of helping them see their buddha nature, and if, while this is being done, you do not notice samādhi, or the form of samādhi, or the cultivator of samādhi, or your potential rewards, good monks, if you can be like this, then you are truly cultivating samādhi.

"And what is cultivation of wisdom? If a cultivator should think like this: 'If I cultivate wisdom for myself alone, then I will quickly achieve liberation and pass beyond the three lower realms. No one can really help all sentient beings, and no one can really save people from the cycle of birth and death. The appearance of a buddha is as rare as an *udumbara* flower. If only I can break my own attachments to suffering, then I will certainly achieve the reward of liberation. For these reasons, I will pursue wisdom to overcome suffering and quickly attain liberation.' One who thinks like this is not truly cultivating wisdom.

"And what is true cultivation of wisdom? If you contemplate that sentient beings are ignorant and that they are trapped in a cycle of birth, old age, death, and suffering, and if you realize that they do not know how to practice the supreme way, and if your realization leads you to vow to use your body of this lifetime to help them with their sufferings, then you are cultivating true wisdom. Sentient beings are weak, greedy, immoral, and base. If you are willing to carry the karma of their greed, anger, and ignorance on your own body, and if you are willing to help them overcome greed, and to help them overcome their attachments to name and form, and to help them become liberated from the cycle of birth and death, and if you are willing to use your body in any way to do this, and if you vow to lead all sentient beings to anuttara-samyak-sambodhi, and if, as you do these things, you do not notice wisdom, or the form of wisdom, or the cultivator of wisdom, or any potential reward, this is true cultivation of wisdom.

"Good monks, the one who cultivates morality, samādhi, and wisdom in these ways is a bodhisattva, while one who is unable to cultivate morality, samādhi, and wisdom in these ways is only a śrāvaka."

CHAPTER TWO

CEASING AND CONTEMPLATING

Ceasing is like clear reflective water
while contemplating is like
the myriad images that
the water reflects.

—from the *Treatise on the*
Completion of Truth

WISDOM AND SAMĀDHI are completely interdependent. Wisdom depends on samādhi, and samādhi depends on wisdom. Buddhist masters conceive of these two states of mind as being inseparable and constantly interacting with each other. Without wisdom there can be no samādhi, and without samādhi there can be no wisdom. The *Mahā-parinirvāṇa Sūtra* says that without the interaction of these two, it is not possible to achieve nirvāṇa.

In Chinese Buddhist practice, the word samādhi is often replaced by the word for ceasing *(chih)* while the word wisdom often is replaced by the word for contemplating *(kuan)*. In Chinese, the Buddhist phrase "equally practicing samādhi and wisdom" means almost the same thing as the phrase "simultaneously cultivating ceasing and contemplating." One could safely say that there is not much difference between the concept of samādhi and the concept of ceasing

in Chinese Buddhism. In the same way, there is little difference between the concept of wisdom and the concept of
contemplating. Samādhi is the ceasing of delusive mental
functions, while wisdom is a state of clear contemplation of
the truth.

"Ceasing and contemplating" or "ceasing-contemplating"
(chih-kuan) is the Chinese name of a fundamental meditation technique. In English, this technique is usually known
by its Sanskrit name *śamatha-vipaśyanā.*

Śamatha means "ceasing delusive thinking." Vipaśyanā
means "contemplating the true nature of all things to overcome suffering."

Since the techniques we will be discussing below have
been honed in China for almost two thousand years, we will
use the term ceasing and contemplating in place of śamatha-
vipaśyanā. By translating this compound word into English,
we have the advantage of keeping our meaning clear and
close at hand. At the same time, we will be better able to keep
some of the distinctions of the Chinese tradition separate
from other meditation traditions that use similar techniques.
Preserving the distinctions between traditions is better for
Buddhism as a whole than trying to blend them into one
generalized tradition. As we go along, it should become
clearer why the Chinese tradition for practical purposes
equates samādhi with ceasing and wisdom with contemplating.

The *Mahāparinirvāṇa Sūtra* says:

> Śamatha is cultivated for three basic reasons: the first is to
> prevent laxity, the second is to discover wisdom, and the
> third is to discover one's natural self. Likewise, vipaśyanā is
> also cultivated for three basic reasons: the first is to con-
> template life, death, and karmic retribution, the second is to

increase the roots of goodness, and the third is to overcome all suffering.

The *Treatise on the Completion of Truth* says:

> Ceasing is the same as samādhi, and contemplation is the same as wisdom. All good dharmas arise from cultivating these two. And why is this so? This is so because ceasing overcomes attachment while contemplating disentangles one entirely from it.

When we cease indulging ourselves in our customary attachments, we gain a momentary respite from their painful bondage. When we contemplate that bondage from this place of momentary cessation, we gain the insight necessary to sever that bond for good. Ceasing and contemplating work together to lift the mind from its lower attachments while helping it find the light of higher awareness.

> *Ceasing is like a weapon*
> *while contemplating is like using*
> *the weapon to capture a thief.*
> —from the *Treatise on the Completion of Truth*

THE RELATIONSHIP BETWEEN CEASING AND CONTEMPLATING

How are ceasing and contemplating interrelated? Ceasing can be thought of as a sort of negative method that seeks to stop the mind from rushing toward its familiar attachments. Contemplating can be thought of as a positive activity that sees things as they really are, without attachment, desire, or

aversion. Properly speaking, ceasing must precede contemplating. If there is no ceasing there can be no contemplating.
This is the reason Buddhist sūtras always discuss samādhi
and ceasing before they discuss wisdom and contemplating.
   The *Mahāparinirvāṇa Sūtra* says:

> If you want to pull up a stubborn weed, you must first grip
> it tightly with your hands; then it will be easy to remove.
> The samādhi and wisdom of a bodhisattva are similar to this.
> First he must grip his defilements with samādhi and then
> he can remove them with wisdom.

   In Buddhist literature there are literally dozens of beautiful
and expressive metaphors designed to help us understand
the important relationship between ceasing and contemplating. The *Treatise on the Completion of Truth* contains
the following very illuminating list of them. The treatise
says that ceasing is like grasping a bunch of grass, while contemplating is like cutting it with a sickle. It says that ceasing
is like sweeping the ground, while contemplating is like
removing manure. It says that ceasing is like wiping something that is dirty, while contemplating is like using water
to wash it. It says that ceasing is like soaking something in
water, while contemplating is like cooking it afterward. It
says that ceasing is like melting gold, while contemplating
is like fashioning a container out of it. It says that ceasing is
like a field, while contemplating is like planting seeds in it.
It says that ceasing is like clear, reflective water, while contemplating is like the myriad images that the water reflects.
It says that ceasing is like standing, while contemplating is
like firing an arrow from that position. It says that ceasing
is like a weapon, while contemplating is like using the
weapon to capture a thief.

The sage sees how to stop clinging
while all others find this very hard.
If you can see through joy and sorrow,
then you too will glimpse the great peace.
　　—from the *Great Treatise on the Perfection of Wisdom*

HOW CEASING AND CONTEMPLATING RELATE TO OTHER BUDDHIST PRACTICES

The basic practice of ceasing and contemplating is so important to Buddhist practice in general that all practices mentioned in the sūtras can be understood in terms of it. In the section below, we will discuss some basic Buddhist practices and show how they are related to ceasing and contemplating.

The thirty-seven conditions leading to buddhahood

These thirty-seven conditions are necessary for becoming a buddha. They are discussed in detail in the Āgamas. In this section, we will merely outline them and show how they are related to ceasing and contemplating.

The first four of the thirty-seven conditions are the *four considerations:*

1) The consideration that the body is unclean. This is an act of ceasing.
2) The consideration that all sense impressions ultimately lead only to suffering. This is an act of ceasing.
3) The consideration that all activities of the mind are impermanent and changeable. This is an act of ceasing.
4) The consideration that all phenomena are interrelated and that none of them has a nature of its own. This is an act of contemplation.

The second four of the thirty-seven conditions leading to buddhahood are the *four exertions*. Each is an act of contemplation. They are considered acts of contemplation because they depend on the discerning wisdom of the mind for their success. The four exertions are:

1) Ending past evil tendencies.
2) Not starting new evil tendencies.
3) Starting good tendencies.
4) Furthering good tendencies that have already started.

The third four of the thirty-seven conditions leading to buddhahood are the *four fulfillments*. Each is an act of ceasing. The four fulfillments are considered acts of ceasing because they depend on samādhi for their fruition. Sometimes the four fulfillments are also called the four steps toward supernatural powers. The four fulfillments are:

1) The fulfillment of desire. In this stage, one's desire for the perfection of one's practice is fulfilled.
2) The fulfillment of diligence or progress. In this stage, one's concentration is perfect and therefore one is able to fulfill all of one's vows.
3) The fulfillment of contemplation or mindfulness. In this stage, one's memory becomes perfect.
4) The fulfillment of thoughtfulness. In this stage, one's mind is perfected and one's thoughts no longer lead one into error.

The *five spiritual roots* are the next stage of the thirty-seven conditions leading to buddhahood. These five roots are the sources of all good dharmas. The five spiritual roots are:

1) The root of faith. When this root is securely planted, it aids all other practices and leads one toward liberation in samādhi without outflows. This is a form of ceasing.
2) The root of diligence. When this root is securely planted, there are no more lapses in one's practice or behavior. This is a form of ceasing.
3) The root of thought. When this root is securely planted, one never forgets the true Dharma. This is a form of ceasing.
4) The root of samādhi. When this root is securely planted, one's samādhi becomes perfect. This is a form of ceasing.
5) The root of wisdom. When this root is firmly planted, one's contemplation of the Dharma is luminous and perfect. This is a form of contemplation.

The *five spiritual powers* are the next stage of the thirty-seven conditions leading to buddhahood. These five powers have the same names and the same relations to ceasing and contemplating as the five roots discussed above. The five spiritual powers are outgrowths of the five spiritual roots.

The *seven degrees of enlightenment* are the next stage of the thirty-seven conditions leading to buddhahood. The seven degrees of enlightenment are:

1) Understanding the Dharma. In this stage, one understands all distinctions between true and false in the Dharma. This is a form of contemplation.
2) Enlightened progress. In this stage, one's progress is continuously informed by one's clear understanding. This is a form of contemplation.
3) Enlightened joy. In this stage, one's enlightenment within the true Dharma begins to produce great joy. This is a form of contemplation.

4) Enlightened non-attachment. In this stage, one is perfectly able to be non-attached to all suffering and all defilement. This is a form of ceasing.

5) Enlightened non-clinging. In this stage, one is free of all clinging to form, view, idea, or any meditative state. This is a form of ceasing.

6) Enlightened samādhi. In this stage, one is able to appreciate fully the enlightening qualities of samādhi. This is a form of ceasing.

7) Enlightened contemplation. In this stage, one understands all means of practice perfectly. This is the only stage of the thirty-seven conditions leading to buddhahood that is considered to be both a stage of ceasing and a stage of contemplating.

The last stage of the thirty-seven conditions leading to buddhahood is the *noble eightfold path*. The eight aspects of the noble eightfold path are:

1) Right views. One can see the truth. This is a form of contemplating.

2) Right thought. The mind is without defilement. This is a form of contemplating.

3) Right speech. This is a form of ceasing.

4) Right action. This is a form of ceasing.

5) Right work. This is a form of ceasing.

6) Right effort. This is a form of contemplating.

7) Right mindfulness. This is a form of ceasing.

8) Right samādhi. This is a form of ceasing.

The thirty-seven conditions leading to buddhahood are a detailed description of the states of mind necessary to attain enlightenment. These conditions are often discussed as "stages," but they should not be understood as actual steps that follow one after the other. In truth, they are more like the facets of a complex and beautiful crystal that can only be seen when they all are gathered together.

> *Contemplate the body until you see its true form.*
> *Then you will cease your grasping.*
> *These contemplations will extinguish the fires of desire*
> *in the same way that torrential rains extinguish wild fires.*
> —from the *Great Treatise on the Perfection of Wisdom*

The seven pure flowers

The *seven pure flowers* are sometimes also called simply the *seven purities*. The seven purities are described in detail in the *Vimalakīrtinirdeśa Sūtra*.

1) Pure morality. One's morality is pure and no defilements remain in the mind. When this state is achieved, one becomes completely fearless. This is a state of ceasing.
2) Pure mind. One's mind is pure and all attachments have been overcome. This is a state of ceasing.
3) Pure views. One's views are in perfect accord with the Dharma and one no longer suffers lapses of selfish or delusive thinking. This is a state of contemplation.
4) Pure doubtlessness. One's understanding of the truth is so deep one has passed completely beyond doubt. This is a state of contemplation.
5) Pure discrimination. One's ability to discriminate between right and wrong is perfect. This is a state of contemplation.
6) Pure equanimity. This is a state of contemplation.
7) Pure nirvāṇa. This is a state of contemplation.

The boundless meanings of the Dharma
all are gathered in purity.

—from the Āgamas

The eight awakenings of the sage

The *eight awakenings of the sage* are the eight great realizations that lead to complete fulfillment in the bodhi mind. The eight awakenings of the sage are described in detail in the *Eight Realizations of the Bodhisattva Sūtra.*

1) The awakening of few desires. In this, the sage realizes that fulfillment of only the most basic bodily needs is all that is necessary to achieve enlightenment. This is a form of ceasing.
2) The awakening of sufficiency. In this, the sage realizes that he can be perfectly satisfied with whatever happens. This is a form of ceasing.
3) The awakening of non-clinging. In this, the sage realizes how to live in the world without clinging to suffering or joy. This is a form of ceasing.
4) The awakening of diligence. In this, the sage realizes how to be diligent in his practice at all times. This is a form of ceasing.
5) The awakening of contemplation. In this, the sage realizes how to think correctly about body, speech, mind, sense impressions, and cultivation of the Dharma. This is a form of ceasing.
6) The awakening of right samādhi. In this, the sage realizes how to achieve proper samādhi. This is a form of ceasing.
7) The awakening of wisdom. In this, the sage fully understands the Dharma. This is a form of contemplation.
8) The awakening of the ending of all idle speech. In this,

the sage puts an end to all mistakes of speech. This is a form of contemplation.

Knowing that sentient beings
all have a thousand desires
gripping the depths of their minds,
the Buddha teaches them
in accordance with their characters and conditions.
With stories, words, and skillful means
he teaches them the truth.
                                            —from the *Lotus Sūtra*

One mind-two doors

The *Avataṃsaka Sūtra* says, "There is no difference between the mind, the Buddha, and all sentient beings."

The *Awakening of Faith in the Mahāyāna* says, "The dharma of one mind has two doors. And what are these two? The first is the *door of the tathāgata* and the second is the *door of phenomenal change*. Together, these two doors are the summation of all dharmas."

The Mind-Only *(Yogācāra)* School of Buddhism holds that the universe and everything in it are nothing more than one great mind, and that all sentient beings and all buddhas are part of this mind. This one great universal mind has enlightened aspects and it has unenlightened aspects, and, for this reason, the Mind-Only School speaks of there being two doors that give access to the truth. The "enlightened door" is the door of the tathāgata, and the "unenlightened door" is the door of phenomenal change.

The door of the tathāgata opens directly onto the enlightened mind, which is beyond phenomenal change, beyond birth and death, beyond increase or decrease, and beyond all duality.

The door of phenomenal change opens onto the unenlightened mind, wherein the phenomenal changes of birth and death, increase and decrease, and all other forms of duality occur.

Buddhist masters speak of *one mind-two doors* to help us comprehend the complex nature of reality. Viewed in one way, everything is Buddha. Viewed in another way, everything that we see is characterized by phenomenal change, suffering, and death.

The door of the tathāgata is the doorway of ceasing. The door of phenomenal change is the doorway of contemplation.

The door of the tathāgata is the doorway of ceasing because this doorway leads beyond delusion, beyond duality, beyond suffering. When one passes through the door of the tathāgata, all distinctions settle into perfect and tranquil wisdom. Metaphorically, we might say that the door of the tathāgata leads directly into the fullness and oneness of the sea, while the door of phenomenal change leads onto the surface of the sea, where the wind blows and whitecaps and waves can appear.

The door of phenomenal change is the doorway of contemplation because this doorway opens onto the phenomenal world with all its dualities and all its many changes. This is the surface of the sea and the plane on which all delusion occurs. If we pass through this door and use our powers of contemplation to understand it, then we quickly learn to dive beneath the surface of phenomenal change and find the source of all things.

The door of the tathāgata is the doorway of ceasing. The door of phenomenal change is the doorway of contemplation. They are two aspects of the same one mind. We can only come to understand the fullness of the one mind by understanding both doors at once.

OTHER KINDS OF CEASING
AND CONTEMPLATING
IN THE CHINESE TRADITION

The Chinese Buddhist tradition is very rich. The truth is always one, but the ways that sentient beings may approach that truth are many. In this section we will discuss four important schools of Chinese Buddhism and briefly describe how they recommend practicing ceasing and contemplating. The four schools we will discuss are the Hua-yen School, the T'ien-t'ai School, the Pure Land School, and the Zen School.

Ceasing and contemplating in the Hua-yen School

The Hua-yen School teaches five kinds of ceasing and contemplating meditation. Master Tu-hsun (557–640) grouped these five kinds of meditation in an order that corresponds to their comparative depth. The shallower techniques are listed first while the deeper ones are listed later. Each technique is one aspect of what is known as Hua-yen samādhi. Hua-yen samādhi is considered to be a complete and perfect samādhi leading to perfect realization of the truth. Hua-yen samādhi is a single-vehicle samādhi. I hope that saying that some of these techniques are deeper than others will not encourage readers to skip the first few techniques in a rush to get to the deepest parts as quickly as possible. Meditative equipoise must be slowly and patiently built up in much the same way that one must slowly and patiently build up the "structure" of any skill. We only hinder ourselves when we ignore fundamentals.

1) *The door of observing phenomena to overcome belief in the*

self. This is a Hīnayāna practice. It is a form of contemplation based on the observation that all phenomena are
produced through the interaction of the five *skandhas,*
the twelve dimensions, and the eighteen realms. By
observing that all things are interconnected and that all
phenomena arise only through the interaction of many
other phenomena, the meditator comes to understand
that he possesses no permanent self whatsoever.

2) *The door of arising and non-arising.* This is a basic Mahāyāna
meditation technique that is used to help the meditator
understand that both phenomena and the self are
empty—that nothing has a self-nature. There are two
ways to perform this meditation.

   a) *Contemplation of non-arising.* In this meditation, the
   meditator contemplates that all things in the universe
   arise only out of the interaction of name and form.
   Phenomena arise solely from the interactions of other
   phenomena, and thus none of them truly arises.

   b) *Contemplation on the emptiness of form.* In this meditation, the meditator contemplates that all phenomena
   are essentially empty—they have no self-nature, they
   do not arise, and they all are impermanent.

3) *The door of uniting basis and form.* This is the same meditation as the one mind-two doors meditation discussed
above. This meditation is one of the most basic kinds of
ceasing and contemplating meditation in Mahāyāna Buddhism. The word basis in the title of this technique is
roughly the same as the words enlightened mind of the
one mind-two doors technique, while the word form is
roughly the same as phenomenal change in the one mind-
two doors technique. As one's study of Buddhism pro-
gresses, one comes to realize that many of the words used
by Buddhist masters are close synonyms. They basically

mean the same thing, but sometimes the use of different words conveys subtle differences. The more experience one has in using these words, the more clearly this point will be understood.

Let me quickly illustrate this point by mentioning the subtle differences between using enlightened mind and basis to describe the same technique. The one mind-two doors viewpoint is a Mind-Only viewpoint, and therefore mind as the basis of all things is emphasized and the term enlightened mind is used. In the Hua-yen School, the viewpoint is not Mind-Only, and therefore a more abstract or generalized word—basis—is chosen to represent the same thing. These subtle distinctions may be ignored if they seem burdensome, or they may be heeded if they seem helpful. Remember that ultimate truth is completely beyond words.

4) *The door of ending both contemplation and language.* This is a technique of the Sudden Enlightenment School. The Sudden Enlightenment School believes that since all sentient beings possess buddha nature, all that one must do is remove all defilements from the surface of that nature to achieve enlightenment. If one can see beyond all language and all belief systems and all contemplations, then one will necessarily attain the perfect vision of liberation. See if you can do it.

5) *Hua-yen samādhi.* This is a complete single-vehicle form of ceasing and contemplating meditation. It is composed of the four techniques described above and may in some ways be thought of as an amalgamation of all of them. In Hua-yen samādhi one contemplates that all phenomena in the universe interact with each other, and that this process of interaction goes on and on without stopping. Things suddenly appear from the confluence of other

things, and then they suddenly disappear again. Stars rise
and fall just as motes of dust circle in the light. The one
is part of the many, and the many are wholly reflected in
the one. They all appear and disappear, and not one of
them obstructs another or permanently grasps any other.

If you want to understand that
all within the three realms
is nothing but buddha mind,
then contemplate that the Dharma realm
is nothing but a product of mind.
    —from the *Avataṃsaka Sūtra*

Ceasing and contemplating in the T'ien-t'ai School

The complete and sudden technique of ceasing and contemplating is one of three important T'ien-t'ai meditation techniques. Since this technique is T'ien-t'ai's most complete
technique, and since it was taught by the great enlightened
Master Chih-i (538–597), we will discuss only this one T'ien-
t'ai method of ceasing and contemplating. The complete
and sudden technique has two parts. Part one is called the
four kinds of samādhi and part two is called the *ten vehicles
of contemplation.* Part one stresses ceasing while part two
stresses contemplation.

1) *The four kinds of samādhi.* Samādhi is a state of perfect
   ceasing. In samādhi, verbal and discursive mental functions
   have ceased, and the mind is filled with wisdom and
   repose. The four kinds of samādhi discussed below are
   excellent methods for achieving perfect ceasing. Once
   perfect ceasing, or samādhi, has been achieved, true contemplation can begin.

a) *Long-sitting samādhi.* The method of long sitting is taken from the *Mañjuśrī-paripṛccha Sūtra* and the *Sūtra of Mañjuśrī's Discourse on Prajñā Wisdom.* This method is quite difficult. It requires the practitioner to spend ninety days in seclusion. During this period, the practitioner should sit continuously in meditation and contemplate the name of a buddha. The single-mindedness that develops from this practice is very strong, and it is capable of overcoming a great deal of bad karma. The intense simplicity of this practice has led to it sometimes being called single-practice samādhi.

b) *Long-walking samādhi.* This method is sometimes also called the *pratyutpanna samādhi* method since it is taken from the *Pratyutpanna-buddha-sammukhāvas-thitā-samādhi Sūtra.* Long-walking samādhi requires the practitioner to spend ninety days in a temple circumambulating an image of the Buddha. No sitting is allowed except during brief meal breaks. As the practitioner walks around the image of the Buddha, he should chant the name of Amitābha Buddha while contemplating the thirty-two signs of his buddhahood. If this practice is performed with concentration and dedication, the practitioner will eventually see a vision of all the buddhas in the universe. For this reason, long-walking samādhi is also known as vision of the buddhas samādhi.

c) *Half-walking half-sitting samādhi.* As its name suggests, this method employs a mixture of walking and sitting. There are two basic kinds of half-walking half-sitting samādhi.

1) *Great universal samādhi.* This practice is taken from the *Great Universal Dhāraṇī Sūtra.* For a period of seven days, the practitioner must confine himself to a temple wherein he chants mantras.

2) *Lotus samādhi.* This practice is taken from the *Mañjughoṣa* and the *Śubhavyūha-rāja* chapters of the *Lotus Sūtra.* For a period of twenty-one days the practitioner engages in chanting, meditating, circumambulating the Buddha, repentance, and other calming practices.

d) *Not-sitting not-walking samādhi.* This practice is taken from the *Mahāprajñāpāramitā Sūtra.* It is not restricted to any time period or any place. This kind of samādhi is supposed to be practiced in the course of our daily lives. Sometimes this samādhi is also called *enlightened awareness samādhi* because it emphasizes mindfulness and contemplation throughout the day. If one performs this practice sincerely and with dedication, one will definitely experience an increase in one's enlightened awareness.

The first three of the above-mentioned practices clearly emphasize strict ceasing and contemplating. Though these practices are difficult, they are very powerful and very effective. The long time periods involved and the arduousness of their physical undertakings make these practices difficult for most modern Buddhists. The last practice mentioned above, however, is perfectly suited for life in the modern world. If we can perform this practice with the same dedication that we might use in undertaking one of the other practices, we will make great progress. Ceasing and contemplating is something we can do overtly with our bodies in the Buddha hall, but it is also something we can do in a less obvious manner in our minds wherever we find ourselves. Though it is regrettable that most of us alive today cannot find ninety continuous days to spend in meditation, none of us should conclude from this that powerful Buddhist practices are unavailable to us. Ceasing and contemplating can and should be done wherever we find ourselves.

The splendor of the tathāgata
is the compassion that dwells
at the center of all minds.
The clothing of the tathāgata
is the gentleness and patience
that dwell in every mind.
The seat of the tathāgata
is the emptiness of all phenomena.
　　　　　　　—from the *Lotus Sūtra*

2) *Ten vehicles of contemplation.* The contemplations that follow are called *vehicles* because they can carry us from this saṃsāric world of suffering to ultimate liberation. The ten vehicles of contemplation are actually ten aspects of one magnificent contemplation. The limitations of words and the tendency of our minds to focus on only one thing at a time, however, forces us to treat them as if they were separate.

a) *Contemplation of the indescribable realm.* In this, the meditator contemplates that every aspect of every moment of life is contingent on the entire universe and that every moment always reflects the awesome bounty and fullness of the entire universe. Once one appreciates that even the most "insignificant" things are an overwhelming part of the entire universe, one cannot but appreciate the indescribable fullness and perfection of the bodhi mind.

b) *Contemplation on the importance of arousing the bodhi mind.* Following the above contemplation, the meditator should recognize that, in general, most of us do not fully appreciate the wonder and awe of bodhi consciousness. Since we do not fully appreciate it, we should contemplate the importance of arousing the bodhi mind.

c) *Ceasing and contemplating with skillful tranquility.* This method asks us to use our own minds to figure out the best way to gain peace and security within the Dharma. No one knows you as well as you know yourself. No one else knows where you are deficient and where you are strong in your practice. This method asks us to be perfectly honest with ourselves and, through this honesty, to grow.

d) *Breaking the hold of all phenomena.* This is an act, a vow, and a form of contemplation all in one. When we break the hold of all phenomena we consider that all attraction and all aversion are fundamentally illusory. Since all attachment is based on illusion, we resolve to break the hold of all of it.

e) *Understanding loss and gain.* This contemplation is sometimes also called understanding obstruction and non-obstruction. This contemplation is used when and if the practitioner recognizes that he has not successfully broken the hold of all phenomena. In this practice, the meditator contemplates the emptiness of all phenomena and the emptiness of both gain and loss. Once one sees that nothing is gained when something is gained and that nothing is lost when something is lost, one will draw closer to being able to overcome one's attachments.

f) *Contemplation of the thirty-seven conditions leading to buddhahood.* This contemplation is used when one realizes that, though one may have broken the hold of all phenomena, one is still not making good progress in other areas. The method used for this practice is to contemplate all of the thirty-seven conditions leading to buddhahood one by one. As one contemplates each of them, one should evaluate oneself and decide where one is still deficient. Once one has determined one's deficiencies, one should contemplate what steps to take to overcome those deficiencies.

As one grows in one's practice and understanding of the Dharma, one must realize that self-reliance and self-understanding are extremely important. Don't always wait for someone else to point out to you how you should improve yourself.

g) *The method of the directed cure.* This method is used to overcome deficiencies that one has identified in oneself. For example, if one has determined that one is lacking in compassion, then one should spend time contemplating compassion. If one has determined that one is lacking in joy, then one should spend time contemplating the importance of joy, both to the self and to others, and one should recognize that joy is a part of true wisdom. Generally speaking, the method for overcoming any particular fault is to stress its positive opposite. Do not dwell on your deficiency. Rather, identify it and stress its opposite. This method is very powerful and no one should ignore it, no matter how advanced they are.

h) *The contemplation of knowing where you really are.* Whenever we think we know more than we do, we close the door to growth. For this reason, it is very important that each one of us determines as accurately as possible where we really are. If you think that you are more advanced in your practice than you really are, you will cause yourself many problems. A poor assessment of your own mind will create a major obstacle to further growth. Generally speaking, it is difficult to be too humble, and thus it is generally better to under-value rather than overvalue ourselves.

i) *Being able to take it.* Our capacity to withstand hard-ship is our greatest tool as well as the best marker we have for the depth of our progress. On a sunny day after a good meal almost anyone can be compassion-ate. Our real test comes when we are called upon to endure hardship with grace and dignity. If you can maintain peace of mind even in adverse situations, then you can be sure that you are making good progress. A word of caution: no one should ever seek out hardship for itself alone. One should willingly face hardship whenever it comes, but no one should ever go looking for it. Our energies are much too valuable to be wasted in pointless exercises like that.

j) *Perfect equanimity.* This contemplation is used to take us beyond all attachment—all attraction and all aversion. This contemplation reveals for us the true middle way, for it shows us the path that travels between all extremes and between all dualities. Eventually, this contemplation will lead us to a state of perfect equa-nimity wherein perfect Dharma patience is born. Once we have achieved Dharma patience, regression on the path is no longer possible.

If you have a scattered mind and are distracted,
enter a temple and call the Buddha's name.
At that moment, you will be back on the path.
　　　　　　　　　　—from the *Lotus Sūtra*

Ceasing and contemplating in the Pure Land School

Pure Land Buddhism, which historically has been the most popular form of Buddhism in East Asia, centers its practice around Amitābha Buddha. Generally speaking, Pure Land Buddhism places more emphasis on the power of Amitābha Buddha to help the practitioner than other Buddhist practices do. Zen and T'ien-t'ai Buddhism, for example, generally place more emphasis on the self-reliance and insight of the practitioner himself.

To be reborn in Amitābha Buddha's pure land is a major goal of Pure Land practitioners. For some practitioners, Amitābha's pure land is conceived of as an actual physical place, while for others it is a more perfectly realized state of mind. The most important feature of Amitābha Buddha's pure land is that it is a buddha realm wherein it is relatively easy to make rapid progress toward enlightenment. All sentient beings there are very worthy, and conditions are perfect for learning the Dharma.

Though China historically produced eight major schools of Buddhism, and though these schools were quite distinct from each other at one time, it is important to understand that there is no *fundamental* difference between them. They are different only in their emphases or in certain of their philosophical interpretations. For this reason, modern Chinese Buddhists generally practice a mixture of techniques from two or more of the eight schools. One of the most effective forms of Buddhist practice is to mix Zen practice with Pure Land practice.

In his *Treatise on Rebirth in the Pure Land,* T'an-luan (476–?) classified six basic Pure Land meditation techniques as being either techniques of ceasing or techniques of contemplation. We will follow his classification below. The six techniques fall into two groups.

1) *The door of vowing.* This is a door of ceasing. Pure Land practice is fundamentally based on the practitioner's vow to be reborn in Amitābha Buddha's pure land. When a practitioner makes this vow, it is very important that he do so with "singleness of mind" or perfect concentration. There are three basic ways to understand this very important vow.

a) The mere act of vowing and repeating Amitābha Buddha's name is enough to cleanse the mind and bring about the cessation of mental defilements.

b) Since the pure land is not part of the three realms, the mere act of being reborn there is enough to cleanse the mind and bring about the cessation of all defilements of body, speech, and mind.

c) The power of Amitābha Buddha's enlightened being itself is so great that he can bring about a cessation in anyone who calls on him.

2) *The door of contemplating.* This is a door of contemplating. In this aspect of Pure Land practice, the practitioner focuses his attention on contemplating, so that he will be successful in overcoming his worldly confusion and habits of delusion. The three basic contemplations are:

a) Contemplating the perfection and magnificence of the pure land.

b) Contemplating the perfection and magnificence of Amitābha Buddha.

c) Contemplating the perfection and magnificence of the bodhisattvas who have taken rebirth in the pure land.

If you want to go to the pure land,
then purify your mind.
When your mind is pure,
then whatever you see will be pure,

and wherever you go
you will find the buddha realm.
—from the *Vimalakīrtinirdeśa Sūtra*

Ceasing and contemplating in the Zen School

Zen Buddhism is one of the most misunderstood of all the schools of Buddhism. Zen is the Japanese pronunciation of the Chinese word *ch'an.* The word ch'an itself is a transliteration of the Sanskrit word dhyāna, which means "meditation" or "absorption." Most Westerners learn of Ch'an or Zen Buddhism from Japanese sources. Japanese Zen Buddhism and Chinese Ch'an Buddhism both have their roots in T'ang Dynasty China. Since the word Zen is more commonly known than the word Ch'an, we will use Zen in our discussion.

Zen Buddhism is based on the idea that, since all sentient beings have a buddha nature, to achieve enlightenment it is only necessary to uncover this buddha within. Since you already are a buddha, you will be enlightened the moment you understand your true nature. I say that Zen is misunderstood because people too often believe that this "uncovering" of the buddha nature within can be achieved without labor. This is not the case. Real Zen practice is highly disciplined, and many years of study must necessarily precede "sudden" liberation in the truth.

In the section below, we will discuss two important Zen meditation techniques and show how they can be understood in terms of ceasing and contemplating.

1) *Contemplation of doubt.* This exceptionally beautiful and effective method uses that weak shiver within our being, our sense of doubt, to raise our awareness. This is a

method of contemplating. The contemplation of doubt is performed by focusing the mind on one's sense of doubt. What do we doubt? As unenlightened beings, we doubt ourselves more deeply than anything else. We doubt that we exist, or that we know anything, or that we can ever possibly know anything. If we focus our mind on this sense of doubt and allow ourselves to follow it, it will eventually lead us to enlightenment. This subtle technique is very powerful.

Without doubt, there can be no enlightenment.
Small doubt leads to small realization,
and great doubt leads to great realization.
— a Zen saying

2) *Hua-t'ou contemplation.* This is a method of contemplation. Hua-t'ou literally means "head of speech" or "source of speech." Hua-t'ou denotes the energy that rises just prior to speech. Hua-t'ou can be understood in two basic ways.

a) Hua-t'ou are often used to stimulate a sense of doubt that can be used in the practice mentioned above. The meditator silently asks himself a question like, "What did my face look like before my parents conceived me?" A sincere attempt to answer this question will quickly lead the mind toward enlightenment. Some other common hua-t'ou questions are "Does a dog have buddha nature?" or "Who is meditating?" or "Who is chanting the Buddha's name?"

b) The hua-t'ou technique is also a very effective method for stilling the mind. Observe yourself and how you speak and listen to language. When someone begins a sentence with the word "if," you may notice that your mind pauses as you wait for them to continue speaking. When this pause after a sentence or a word is deliberately brought into the mind and extended, it is another form of hua-t'ou practice. Some people who have tried for years to quiet their minds in meditation without success succeed very quickly with this technique. Hua-t'ou used in this way might almost be called a form of contemplation and ceasing rather than ceasing and contemplation.

*Before samādhi, the mountains were mountains
and the streams were streams.
In samādhi, the mountains were not mountains
and the streams were not streams.
After samādhi, the mountains were mountains
and the streams were streams again.*
                                        —a Zen saying

CONCLUSION

When we think of meditation, we mostly think of sitting meditation. Sitting meditation is the right way to begin serious practice of ceasing and contemplating, but it is important to remember that ultimately ceasing and contemplating should be practiced throughout the day, no matter what we are doing. Great meditation masters always stress this point. If we have wisdom only when we are alone in a secluded place, our wisdom cannot be very deep. Buddhism must be practiced in this world, wherever we find ourselves. If we understand karma deeply and if we understand the bodhi realization that everything is as it should be, then we will also fully understand that every moment provides us with the very conditions that are most beneficial to us. If our practice of ceasing and contemplating is strong, everything that happens to us will help us grow.

Ceasing and contemplating is one aspect of the three trainings discussed in chapter 1. The practice of ceasing and contemplating depends completely on the three trainings for its success.

Though we speak of the three trainings and the dual aspects of ceasing and contemplating, it is important to remember that we talk this way only because words have their limitations. A good practitioner should understand that the three trainings and ceasing and contemplating are always practiced together. They are different aspects of the same thing. Together they form a kind of vehicle that can carry us very far. No one can say that one wheel of this vehicle is more important than the others—the vehicle is the sum of its parts and it is more than the sum of its parts. Without all of its parts it cannot move forward efficiently. To explain a point, we call this practice a vehicle. In truth, however, it is an inner attitude and an inner resolve. The decisions we make deep within ourselves are the ones that truly carry us forward.

Do no evil ever.
Do good always.
Purify your mind.
These are the teachings of all buddhas.

CHAPTER THREE

THE EIGHT
DHYĀNAS

PROGRESS AND GROWTH in Buddhism follow the general
principles of progress and growth in any field. First we
learn the basics and then we build more complex skills on
them. Buddhist morality begins with the five precepts. Only
after a practitioner has learned to abide by the five basic
precepts should he consider taking the ten precepts or the
bodhisattva vow.

The study of meditation is the same. First we must learn
the basics. Once we know how to sit and calm our minds, we
can begin to learn how to approach deep states of samādhi.

Buddhist meditation masters have arranged eight major
kinds of meditative absorption, or dhyāna, in the order of
their depth and difficulty. For the most part, each level is
built on top of the levels that come before it, though of
course glimpses of higher levels are possible at any time.

The eight dhyānas *(ting)* is a general name for two groups
of four dhyānas each. The first and more basic group of four
dhyānas is usually called the four ch'an in Chinese. These
four dhyānas, or ch'an states, do not transcend the form

realm *(rūpadhātu)*. The second group of four dhyānas does transcend the form realm. In these dhyāna states, the meditator enters the formless realm *(arūpadhātu)*. Saṃsāra is a general term for the deluded state of the human mind. Saṃsāra is comprised of three realms: the form realm, the formless realm, and the desire realm. Most people spend most of their time in the desire realm. Whenever we achieve a meditative state in which all desire drops away, we have left the desire realm and entered the form realm or the formless realm. Since desire is so strong in human beings, any meditative state in which desire falls away is called dhyāna.

In the form realm there is no desire, but the mind retains its capacity to experience enjoyment. In contrast, the formless realm is an entirely spiritual realm. The form realm is the realm of dhyāna heaven while the formless realm is the realm of the highest four heavens. The form realm can be entered through the first four of the eight dhyānas, while the formless realm can be entered only through the last four of the eight dhyānas. The very highest levels of meditation transcend all three of these realms.

The first four of the eight dhyānas are an essential basis for higher wisdom. These states are very stable, and in them one is able to contemplate and understand many things. In contrast, the second four of the eight dhyānas are very subtle. These are states of extreme absorption wherein little or no contemplative activity occurs. All eight of these dhyāna states are very important. In our discussion below, each dhyāna state will be discussed from an objective and a subjective point of view.

THE FIRST FOUR
OF THE EIGHT DHYĀNAS

1) The first dhyāna

a) *The objective point of view.* This first dhyāna is already beyond the desire realm. One can identify this state by the absence of desire. Though desire is gone, the mind still thinks in this state. The thinking that is characteristic of this state can be understood as having two sides or aspects. The first side is comparatively blunt or crude, while the second side is comparatively subtle or refined. The first kind of thinking might be called searching, while the second kind might be called examining. First we search for something and then, when we have found it, we examine it.

These delicate and beautiful distinctions can be expressed in metaphors. In the *Abhidharma-skandha-pāda Śāstra*, the searching and examining aspects of the mind are compared to the ringing of a bell. The searching aspect is like the first blunt sound that issues from a bell when it is struck, while the examining aspect is like the pure musical ringing that trails after that. The *Abhidharma-skandha-pāda Śāstra* also compares the searching and examining aspects of the mind to a bird taking off in flight. The śāstra says that the searching aspect is like the first powerful beatings of a bird's wings, while the examining aspect is like the leap that launches it into flight.

In this dhyāna one has passed beyond the senses of smell and taste, but one still retains the senses of sight, hearing, touch, and thought. It is within these four senses or states of consciousness that the joy of this dhyāna occurs. (Buddhism recognizes six basic states of saṃsāric awareness. These six states or senses are called consciousnesses in Buddhism. They are the consciousnesses of sight, hearing, smell, taste, touch, and thought.)

b) *The subjective point of view.* In this state, the meditator feels joyful and tranquil. The breath feels as if it is coming and going through all of the pores of the body. The joy of this state is completely removed from any sense of pleasure or happiness that is dependent on gaining something in the desire realm.

2) The second dhyāna

a) *The objective point of view.* In this dhyāna, one has passed beyond the kind of thinking described in the first dhyāna. The mind is balanced, even, and calm. This state is the primary source of deep faith and it generally arrives only after a meditator has fully explored the first dhyāna and begun to understand that, though it is wonderful, even more is possible.

In this dhyāna, one has passed beyond the senses of sight, hearing, and touch, but the sense or consciousness of thought still remains.

b) *The subjective point of view.* Bliss is born in this dhyāna. Bliss springs from this dhyāna. In this dhyāna the mind has suddenly opened wide and is filled with a brilliant light. In the first dhyāna, the mind feels like it is shut in a quiet room. In this dhyāna, the mind feels like it has suddenly gone outdoors and seen the sun and moon for the first time.

3) The third dhyāna

a) *The objective point of view.* This dhyāna is characterized by non-clinging. This detached non-clinging, or non-attachment, provides the ground for the further growth of right mindfulness and right concentration.

Incidentally, it is important to understand that the Buddhist terms detached, non-clinging, and non-attachment do not imply negative, apathetic states of mind. Quite the contrary, the non-clinging state is the very state of mind wherein the deepest forms of compassion are born. In Chinese, the word for detachment *(she)* can sometimes also mean "bestow" or "give."

In this dhyāna, of the six basic senses, only thought consciousness in a very pure form remains.

b) *The subjective point of view.* In this dhyāna, the mind passes beyond any attachment to its own entrancing wonders. The mind is filled with joy, but it does not cling to that joy, and it does nothing whatever to seek it.

Buddhists masters sometimes call this dhyāna the "greatest joy of this world." In this state, for the first time, the meditator has passed completely beyond searching for joy or clinging to joy. The joy that results from this is thus pure and undefiled.

4) The fourth dhyāna

a) *The objective point of view.* This dhyāna is almost entirely free of all thought consciousness. The merest trace of movement between receiving and abandoning thoughts occurs. During this dhyāna, breathing stops entirely.

b) *The subjective point of view.* This dhyāna is beyond joy. This is the purest of the first four dhyānas. In this state, the mind is like a spotless mirror reflecting nothing or like a body of water that is perfectly still and undisturbed by the slightest wave. The fourth dhyāna is sometimes also called the "first true dhyāna."

Śākyamuni Buddha said that nirvāṇa is based on the first four dhyānas described above. Approaching and entering these dhyānas is an important part of Buddhist practice.

After these dhyāna states have been experienced and fully explored, the practitioner will begin to understand that still higher and purer states of awareness are possible. The first four dhyānas are marked by some interaction with the form realm and thus they cannot be completely satisfying. In these states one experiences a taste of, but not full, liberation.

When one contemplates
sickness, old age, and death,
one sees that no one and nothing
can escape them.
When compassion is born
in the heart,
one sees that there is no reason
to add to the evil and pain.
    —from the *Great Treatise on the Perfection of Wisdom*

THE SECOND FOUR OF THE EIGHT DHYĀNAS

1) Emptiness without boundaries

a) *The objective point of view.* This dhyāna is beyond both the desire realm and the form realm. The mind dwells in the formless realm and has completely transcended the three basic forms: observable relative forms; non-observable relative forms; and non-observable, non-relative forms. In this dhyāna, the mind faces emptiness directly and nothing intervenes.

b) *The subjective point of view.* The mind has penetrated

emptiness and is clear and pure. There is even less attachment and movement in this state than in the preceding dhyāna. One feels like a bird that has been released from a cage. The panorama is breathtaking.

2) Consciousness without boundaries

a) *The objective point of view.* In this dhyāna, all mental conditions become completely and entirely empty. The sudden vastness of the emptied mind is so huge, however, that a tremor of instability will begin to shake it. This tremor alerts the mind to its need to look into itself for the sources of all relative phenomena. Once these inner sources are understood, one will no longer have any attachment to anything outside of oneself. In the fullness of this awesome awareness, one will transcend time and see clearly and in detail all mental events from the past, the present, and the future. Though these events will appear in the mind, they will not in any way disturb its perfect equanimity.

b) *The subjective point of view.* The mind is clear, tranquil, empty, and aware. The events of the paragraph above seem to happen of themselves.

3) Non-localized dhyāna

a) *The objective point of view.* In this dhyāna, the mind is so free of conditions it has no location.

b) *The subjective point of view.* Boundless tranquility and vast emptiness. The events of past, present, and future perceived in the previous dhyāna are themselves fundamentally empty. As the mind realizes this, it tends to cling to a sense of location. When this clinging to a sense of location is overcome, non-localized dhyāna occurs.

4) The dhyāna of not thinking and not not thinking

a) *The objective point of view.* In this dhyāna, the mind

has gone beyond even not thinking to a state called "not thinking and not not thinking." These terms are not meant to be confusing. Buddhist masters have carried human consciousness so far beyond the limits of language that there really is no way to use language to describe what they have found. We all know what thinking is, and most of us know what not thinking is. The dhyāna described here is a state of awareness that is well beyond both states. In addition to transcending all possible dualities of thought, this dhyāna also transcends all possible dualities of location, form, and mental activity. This is the highest state of dhyāna possible within the three realms.

b) *The subjective point of view.* The mind sees beyond existence and non-existence in a state of immense tranquility. Virtually all parameters of a separate self have been transcended in this dhyāna.

When the sun rises,
stars disappear from the sky.
    —from the *Great Treatise on the Perfection of Wisdom*

CONCLUSION

The eight dhyānas were taught by Śākyamuni Buddha. They are an integral part of Buddhist practice and should not be ignored by anyone who wants to practice Buddhism fully. True wisdom is found in these states and is based on these states. The eight dhyānas are like the steps one climbs toward nirvāṇa. If these dhyāna states are diligently pursued by one who is well grounded in the three trainings, the very deepest secrets of life will be revealed.

In pursuing these dhyāna states, it is important to remember that a higher level is generally attained only after one has fully explored and become slightly dissatisfied with the level below it. This process of exploration and growth can only move forward if one is diligent and unrelenting in one's practice. Growth in dhyāna states is highly dependent on a constant and consistent application of energy. If we decide to rest or to quit before we have reached the highest levels, we will quickly slide backwards and lose most of our gains. The path of growth in dhyāna is beautiful and exhilarating, but no one should believe that it is easy or that it can be traveled without really trying.

Buddhist masters use metaphors to make this point. They say that study is like rowing a boat upstream: to stop is to float backward. Or they say that study is like boiling water over a fire: if you do not tend the fire and keep adding wood to it, the water will never boil.

The *Mahāprajñāpāramitā Sūtra* says that the highest level of dhyāna is the pāramitā of concentration. This pāramitā completely transcends all selfishness. At this level the meditator understands completely that enlightened consciousness is compassionate consciousness.

In this dhyāna one does not accept selfish pleasures,
one does not seek any reward, and one is not moved
by karmic rewards. One enters dhyāna solely for the
purpose of establishing one's mind. And then, out of
wisdom, one returns to life in the desire realm for the
purpose of helping all sentient beings achieve liberation.
This dhyāna is called the pāramitā of concentration.
　　　　　　—from the *Mahāprajñāpāramitā Sūtra*

CHAPTER FOUR

THE FIVE
CONTEMPLATIONS

THE FIVE CONTEMPLATIONS are the contemplation on uncleanness, the contemplation on compassion, the contemplation on conditioned arising, the contemplation on Buddha, and the contemplation on breathing. In Mahā-yāna Buddhism these five contemplations are considered to be essential foundations for the pāramitā of concentration.

Generally speaking, the five contemplations are used to cure specific problems. The contemplation on uncleanness is used to cure greed. The contemplation on compassion is used to cure anger. The contemplation on conditioned arising is used to cure ignorance. The contemplation on Buddha is used to cure attachment. The contemplation on breathing is used to cure scattered thinking.

When using one of the five contemplations to correct a spiritual problem, it is very important that the right contemplation be employed. It is also very important that the contemplation be changed once the problem has been worked on long enough. For example, the contemplation on compassion is appropriate for a person who is suffering from the disease of anger, but it is inappropriate for a person who is suffering from the disease of greed. Compassion overcomes anger, but in some cases it can increase greed. Similarly, the contemplation on uncleanness is appropriate for a person who is suffering from greed, but it is inappropriate for a person who is suffering from anger since this contemplation may only exacerbate the problem. For someone who is suffering from both greed and anger, the right balance must be struck between these two contemplations. This is an area where it is very beneficial to seek out the advice of others.

CONTEMPLATION ON UNCLEANNESS

This contemplation is a graphic reminder of our impermanence and of the futility of seeking happiness solely in the things of this world. When we apply this contemplation to our own bodies, we help ourselves overcome all attachments to the flesh. When we apply this contemplation to the bodies of others, we do so principally to overcome sexual desire."

The *Lotus Sūtra* says, "The cause of all suffering is greed." Without the illusion of self, greed cannot survive. By opposing this illusion with a vision of decrepitude, we go a long way toward overcoming greed itself.

The contemplation on uncleanness is mentioned many times in Buddhist sūtras. This contemplation can generally be divided into three basic types: contemplation on one's own uncleanness, contemplation on the uncleanness of others, and contemplation on the uncleanness of everything in the phenomenal world. We will discuss each of these types below.

Contemplation on one's own uncleanness

The body is sometimes called a "foul bag" in Buddhism to remind us of its impermanence and the futility of vainly preening its every need. The following five methods are designed to help us break free of our deluded entrancements with ourselves.

1) Contemplate that the very seeds of your being are unclean. A body is also called a "retribution body" in Buddhism because a body can be produced only if karmic seeds of retribution are present. We contain those karmic seeds inside us. In addition, our bodies originate from our parents' unclean ovum and semen.

2) Contemplate that your life in this world began with a nine-month stay in your mother's unclean womb.

3) Contemplate that the make-up of your body is unclean— it is formed from skin, bones, blood, lymph, and flesh, and it maintains itself through the operation of fundamentally unclean organs.

4) Contemplate that the outside of your body is unclean. It has hair, nails, teeth, and peeling skin. It sweats, defecates, urinates, salivates, and produces mucous, and if you do not wash it every day, it smells bad and feels worse.

5) Contemplate that, as bad as all the above is, it gets worse after death. After death the body swells up and rots. It bursts with filthy liquids if left unburied or unburned.

Contemplations on the uncleanness of others

These contemplations are the same as the foregoing ones except that they are directed toward the bodies of others. They are designed primarily to help us overcome sexual attraction. The *Yogācārabhūmi Śāstra* and the *Abhidhar-makośa* both divide sexual attraction into four basic categories. If we are able to understand what it is that is making us feel sexually aroused, we will be in a much better position to overcome it. Once we understand the causes of our desires, we can overcome them by contemplating their uncleanness. The śāstras say sexual attraction is caused by one or more of the following:

1) Sexual attraction inspired by physical coloring. This includes hair and skin color, make-up, clothing, and so forth.
2) Sexual attraction inspired by physical shape. This includes height, weight, beauty, appearance, and so forth.
3) Sexual attraction inspired by touch.
4) Sexual attraction inspired by behavior and mannerisms. This includes all behavior, tone of voice, gesture, and so forth.

When we pay close attention to the origins of sexual attraction, we are better prepared to contemplate its essentially delusive nature.

Contemplation on the uncleanness of everything in the phenomenal world

1) Contemplate that everything that we perceive is produced by the confluence of our minds with the conditions of our lives. Whenever we become attached either to some aspect of our minds or to some aspect of the conditions in which we find ourselves, we begin sowing new seeds of karmic uncleanness. The desire realm is the lowest of the three realms. Every time we allow ourselves to be seduced by it, we increase our attachment to it.

2) Contemplate that all greed that arises from form is fundamentally unclean. Form can be understood to be unclean through contemplating higher realms and comparing it to them. Even slight inklings of the much more spiritual formless realm can be very useful in helping us overcome attachment to the form realm. Similarly, comparing the form realm to nirvāṇa can help us overcome the sense that we really must have what our greed says we must have.

3) Contemplate that the phenomenal world is completely conditioned by suffering and impermanence. The three realms are like a vast burning building. All that happens within them is impermanent and fundamentally painful. This contemplation is very helpful for overcoming selfishness and the crude greed that stems from it.

> *Be correct in your behavior*
> *and do good things.*
> *Keep your body clean*
> *and practice well*
> *to cleanse the defilements of your mind.*
> *Be honest and true*
> *in your speech and in your actions*
> *and keep your inner and outer selves the same,*
> *for goodness brings liberation.*
> —from the *Sukhāvatīvyūha Sūtra*

CONTEMPLATION ON COMPASSION

This contemplation is used primarily to overcome anger and all of the negative emotions associated with it. Anger is a negative mental state that seeks to harm others. Sometimes this harm is obvious, and sometimes it can be very subtle. Meanness, pettiness, selfishness, resentment, rudeness, and many other base emotions are frequently caused by the basic emotion of anger. Sometimes one of the more difficult aspects of overcoming anger is recognizing it at all. There are three kinds of contemplation on compassion used to overcome anger.

Contemplation of compassion based on the conditions of life

This contemplation is recommended for people who suffer from sudden and unreasonable bursts of anger that seem to have no real cause. Buddhists call this kind of anger "unreasonable" or "perverse" anger to distinguish it from other forms. The contemplation used to overcome unreasonable anger is done in steps: first one contemplates a loved one or someone whom one cares about and imagines them in a state of happiness. Following that, one contemplates someone toward whom one feels neutral and imagines them in a state of happiness. Then, one contemplates someone toward whom one feels angry and imagines them in a state of happiness. Lastly, one contemplates all sentient beings and imagines them all in a state of happiness.

Contemplation of compassion based on the Dharma

This contemplation is used to cure what is called "reasonable" anger. Reasonable anger is anger felt toward someone who is behaving immorally or who is deliberately trying to cause us trouble. One practices this contemplation by considering that all sentient beings are fundamentally empty—that is, they all lack a permanent self-nature. All beings are interconnected and interdependent, and in the end all beings are one. There is no real distinction between one being and another. Once this truth has been glimpsed, we should imagine sharing the peace and joy we have learned in meditation with whomever is causing us to feel angry. Gradually, we will find that our anger subsides.

Contemplation of compassion based on transcending conditions

Contemplating this kind of compassion is used to overcome what is called "argumentative" anger. Argumentative anger is anger that is caused by hearing someone assert an opinion that is different from our own. Argumentative anger can be overcome by contemplating that all distinctions are fundamentally empty and that all products of the discursive mind are fundamentally deluded. Since all dualistic thought is fundamentally deluded, there should be no reason whatsoever to become angry when someone says something we do not agree with.

> Give benefit and joy
> to all sentient beings.
> Foster their goodness and protect it,
> and blend with it in order to teach them.
> Practice the bodhi way and use good words,
> and you will never become fatigued.
> —from the *Pravara-deva-rāja-paripṛccha Sūtra*

CONTEMPLATION
ON CONDITIONED ARISING

Conditioned arising is sometimes also called "dependent arising," "dependent origination," or "co-dependent origination." Conditioned arising means that all phenomena arise from other phenomena or conditions. Nothing arises on its own. Since all phenomena are interconnected, no one phenomenon can be said to have its own nature. The interconnectedness of all phenomena is one of the three Dharma seals that "stamp" all phenomena. The other two Dharma seals are impermanence and nirvāṇa.

The contemplation on conditioned arising is used primarily to overcome ignorance. The Buddha taught that the three poisons that prevent us from seeing the truth are greed, anger, and ignorance. These poisons are spoken of as if they were three separate and distinct things, but the truth is they are but one thing, for ignorance is the foundation of all delusion. Without ignorance, neither greed nor anger could survive for a single moment.

Ignorance means not knowing. Whenever we form views without knowing the fullness of the truth, we are ignorant. The views that we form out of ignorance can range from relatively simple mistaken views all the way to severe psychopathy. All of us who have not achieved full enlightenment are ignorant in one way or another, and thus all of us should pay careful attention to every means available for overcoming ignorance. There are three basic contemplations on conditioned arising, as discussed below.

Contemplation on the three periods of time and the twelve causal conditions

Śākyamuni Buddha became enlightened through contemplation of the twelve causal conditions. In the Āgamas the Buddha summarized the workings of the twelve causal conditions as follows:

Because there is this, therefore there is that.
This arises and therefore that arises.
If this does not exist, then that will not exist.
If this is extinguished, then that will be extinguished.

This means that the twelve causal conditions give rise to the phenomenal world in a definite order. The first causal condition gives rise to the second causal condition, while the second causal condition gives rise to the third, and the third to the fourth and so on. If the first causal condition is removed, then none of the rest will arise.

The twelve causal conditions are known in Sanskrit as the twelve *nidānas*. In English, they are sometimes called the twelve links in the chain of existence. In order they are: ignorance, activity, awareness, name and form, the six sense awarenesses (eye, ear, nose, tongue, body, mind), touch or contact, feeling or sensation, desire, grasping, having or being, birth, and death.

The first causal condition is ignorance. Contemplation of the twelve causal conditions leads to the eradication of ignorance and thus to the eradication of all of the twelve nidānas. When all of the twelve nidānas have been eradicated, the mind will be completely enlightened.

The contemplation we are discussing now is called the "contemplation on the three periods of time and the twelve causal conditions" because an essential aspect of the twelve causal conditions is that they operate within the three periods of time. The three periods are the past, present, and future.

The first two of the twelve causal conditions—ignorance and activity—are associated with the past. Microcosmically, these two causal conditions gave rise to you. Macrocosmically, they gave rise to the universe. Without ignorance, there would have been no activity. Without activity, there would have been none of the rest of the phenomenal world. Without ignorance there would be nothing but enlightened awareness, nothing but the buddha mind.

The next eight of the twelve causal conditions are associated with the present. Microcosmically, they are the causal conditions that produce and sustain you. Macrocosmically, they are the causal conditions that produce and sustain the universe.

The last two of the twelve causal conditions—birth (or rebirth) and death—are associated with the future. Contemplating these two causal conditions can help us understand that all phenomena are impermanent.

The *Mahāyānābhidharma-samuccaya-vyākhyā Śāstra* separates contemplation on the three periods of time and the twelve causal conditions into four basic types:

a) *Contemplation going with the flow of the many-varied causal conditions.* This contemplation begins with the consideration that primal ignorance and activity are the fundamental causes of all delusion and of all of the rest of the twelve causal conditions. This contemplation begins at the beginning and flows from there.

b) *Contemplation going against the flow of the many-varied causal conditions.* This contemplation begins with contemplation of death and then works backward to consider the many sources and causes of delusion. The *Mahāyānābhi-dharma-samuccaya-vyākhyā Śāstra* uses the term "many-varied causal conditions" in the names of these four contemplations to emphasize the extremely disordered and confusing process that produces and sustains the delusive world. Śākyamuni Buddha understood that delusion is fundamentally created out of only twelve causal conditions. He also understood, however, that the interaction of these twelve causal conditions is extremely complex. Thus, in contemplating this interaction, it is helpful to think of it as being disordered, confused, and "many varied."

c) *Pure contemplation going with the flow of the many-varied causal conditions.* This contemplation begins with the understanding that if ignorance is eradicated, then activity and all of the other twelve causal conditions also will be eradicated. This contemplation begins with a glimpse of enlightenment and then flows forward in perfect purity from there.

d) *Pure contemplation going against the flow of the many-varied causal conditions.* This contemplation begins with the understanding that if death can be overcome, then rebirth also can be overcome. This contemplation begins with the last of the twelve causal conditions and works backward from there, erasing the delusive causes that lead to death in the first place.

The contemplation on the three periods of time and the twelve causal conditions is used primarily to help cure the delusions of nihilism and eternalism. The nihilist sees that nothing is permanent, but he does not realize that a higher awareness lies beyond this initial vision. In contrast, the eternalist sees that there is more to life than meets the eye, but he does not realize that nothing can exist forever. Practicing the contemplation on the three periods of time and the twelve causal conditions can overcome both of these delusions and their root cause—ignorance.

Contemplation on karmic fruits and the twelve causal conditions

This contemplation is used to help overcome the delusion that phenomena have a real, true existence. Insofar as one believes that phenomena have a real, true existence, one will develop attraction or aversion toward them. This attraction or aversion is a very powerful form of ignorance. It leads immediately to the planting of karmic seeds, which eventually grow and produce karmic fruits. In doing this contemplation, one should recognize the inevitability of karmic forces, while at the same time recognizing that even they are fundamentally empty. Delusion causes suffering; the way out of delusion is to understand that even suffering is a delusion. By often practicing the contemplation on karmic fruits and the twelve causal conditions, the paradoxical nature of delusion and liberation will gradually become clear, and one's tendency to feel aversion or attraction for the things of this saṃsāric world will diminish.

Contemplation on a moment of thought and the twelve causal conditions

Some people are quite good at thinking and arguing. This ability deludes them into believing that they know more than they really do. The strength of their mind deludes them into believing that what they are thinking about has an independent self-nature. They believe that their thoughts are real and that their thoughts are actually concerned with some reality that exists independently of them. This delusion

is called the "delusion of believing in a self-existent world."
This delusion is based fundamentally on an error that can
be perceived in any moment of thought. In practicing the
contemplation on a moment of thought and the twelve
causal conditions, one should consider that all of the twelve
causal conditions are present in every moment, and thus
they are present in every moment of thought. By contemplating this, one will come to understand that each and every
moment of thought is intimately and intricately interwoven
within the matrix of the entire universe. Each thought is the
universe. If a thought is founded on false assumptions, a
false and delusive universe will result. If a thought is founded on truth, enlightened understanding will result.

Śākyamuni Buddha taught the twelve causal conditions
to help us understand the very foundation of sentient delusion. It is important to understand that these twelve causal
conditions operate with great speed. In a flash, they all fire
almost at once. Only a highly adept meditator can begin to
perceive any separation between them. The contemplation
on a moment of thought and the twelve causal conditions
is excellent for people who are deluded by the intricacy and
strength of their minds more than by laziness or a tendency
to accept conventional ideas without giving them proper
consideration.

All phenomena are produced by causal conditions.
This is the law of confluence.
This law itself, however,
does not have a definite form,
and thus it too is empty.
—from the *Great Treatise on the Perfection of Wisdom*

CONTEMPLATION ON BUDDHA

This contemplation is used primarily to diminish bad karma. The conditions of our present lives are a product of the general conditions of the world and our own past actions. The general conditions of the world are a product of all the karma of all the people in the world. Karma is produced through intentional acts—good karma results from good actions, and bad karma results from bad actions. Since all sentient beings are interrelated, the karma of other sentient beings also affects each one of us. The repercussions of our own past actions, however, are naturally much greater for us than the repercussions of other people's actions.

Strictly speaking, there is no such thing as "bad" or "good" karma, since karma is itself nothing but a neutral law of cause and effect. Both in Chinese and English, however, people frequently use the short phrases bad karma and good karma instead of the longer phrases bad karmic seeds or good karmic fruits. As long as karma is understood to be a law, the shorter phrases used in Chinese and English are very good ways of expressing the effects of karma because, at the individual level, karmic influences are often actually felt as forces or energies that seem to come from nowhere. Suddenly we feel the need to move, or suddenly we feel angry or happy—these are karmic forces manifesting themselves in our lives, these are karmic seeds beginning to grow.

It is important to understand the powerful and uncontrollable force of karma. Even a buddha cannot change the laws of karma. A buddha can, however, help us diminish the force of karma, and a buddha can help us destroy bad karmic seeds that we ourselves planted some time in the past.

The contemplation on Buddha is used primarily to

diminish bad karma. This contemplation is very important for practicing Buddhists because the nature of karma is such that, once one begins to improve oneself, negative karmic forces stored as seeds in the *ālaya* consciousness begin to sprout more quickly. It is almost as if there were an elasticity in karma—as one stretches toward the good, evil pulls one back with increased force. Another way of looking at this same situation is to say that as we become quieter, even slight noises bother us more. Or, as we become wiser, ignorance appears even more widespread than before. Or, as we become purer, our temptations seem to increase. In clear water, even a little muck catches the eye.

The contemplation on Buddha is used to overcome these problems. There are three basic types of contemplation on Buddha.

1) *Contemplation on the brilliant nirmāṇakāya of Buddha.* The earthly body of a buddha is called his nirmāṇakāya. A buddha has three bodies: an earthly body, which can be seen by sentient beings; a "body of delight," which can be seen only by highly advanced bodhisattvas; and a spiritual body, which is beyond form. The Buddha's body of delight is called his *sambhogakāya*. His spiritual body is called *dharmakāya*.

Contemplation on the brilliant nirmāṇakāya of Buddha is used to overcome torpor, sleepiness, unclear thinking, or laziness. By contemplating the body of the Buddha as he lived and worked in this world, we can learn how to live ourselves in this world. This contemplation is usually practiced by contemplating each one of the thirty-two physical marks that distinguish a buddha from ordinary sentient beings. Generally, the point between the Buddha's eyes is contemplated first. One should visualize a

brilliant light emanating from this point. This light gives
strength, peace, and wisdom to all who try to see it.

2) *Contemplation on the magnificence of Buddha's sambhogakāya.* Sambhogakāya literally means "reward body."
A buddha obtains a reward body because he has earned
it. All buddhas begin as ordinary beings. They distinguish
themselves through the extra effort they expend in seeking the truth. A buddha's sambhogakāya can only be seen
by highly advanced bodhisattvas, though the rest of us
can contemplate its perfection in order to calm our minds
and purge them of negative urges. The nirmāṇakāya of a
buddha is projected into the world through the compassionate meditation of his or her sambhogakāya.

The contemplation on the magnificence of Buddha's
sambhogakāya is generally used to overcome evil
thoughts, immoral desires, and taking delight in evil
things.

This contemplation is practiced by contemplating the
magnificent perfection of Buddha—his fearlessness, his
loving-kindness, his all-knowing wisdom, his calmness,
and his infinite compassion. By frequently contemplating
these magnificent attributes, we foster a healthy sense of
shame in ourselves. Seeing ourselves in comparison to
Buddha helps us learn to regret our evil thoughts and
desires. His magnificence inspires us to redouble our
efforts to improve ourselves.

3) *Contemplation on the emptiness and inactivity of a buddha's dharmakāya.* The dharmakāya is the spiritual body
of a buddha. Dharmakāya is a near synonym for buddha
nature. When we speak of the buddha within each and
every sentient being, we are speaking of the dharmakāya.
There are many buddhas in the universe, but at this level
of abstraction there is only one buddha and everything is

buddha. All things are buddha and all things are seen and known by buddha. The dharmakāya is beyond time, beyond form, beyond attribute, and beyond all duality.

The contemplation on the emptiness and inactivity of the dharmakāya is used principally to overcome negative worldly conditions, such as medically untreatable pain, visions of evil spirits, nightmares, and psychological agony. These conditions result from the forces of the world around us impinging on us too strongly. They can be overcome by contemplating the permanence, the peace, and the perfect equanimity of the dharmakāya.

Since the dharmakāya is beyond all duality, we say that it is empty. Since it pervades everything and is everywhere at all times, we say that it is inactive. Since it is beyond time and space, we say that it is formless. The dharma-kāya is within you. By contemplating its all-pervasiveness and its perfection, you will be greatly helped in overcoming the pressures of delusion and the pain that delusion causes.

Hold the Buddha's name close to you
and you will know no fear
and no weakness in your heart.
—from the *Twelve Names of the Buddha Sūtra*

CONTEMPLATION ON THE BREATH

The full name of this contemplation is "contemplation on counting the breath." In Sanskrit, this meditation technique is called *anāpāna*. Anāpāna is one of the most fundamental and powerful of all the many meditation techniques. In Sanskrit, *ana* means inhale and *apāna* means exhale. Anāpāna gains its strength from its simplicity and from its ability to lead the mind quickly into one-pointed concentration. Perfect concentration on the flow of the breath is a doorway that opens, almost immediately, onto the vast stretches of higher awareness. This technique should not be ignored by anyone who wants to find the truth.

Anāpāna is the basis of the contemplation on counting the breath. By first counting our breath and then actively contemplating the process of breathing, we can quickly learn to overcome scattered thinking and the frailties attendant on mental disorganization. The Chinese tradition recognizes six basic stages of contemplating the breath: actually counting the breath, mentally following the breath, ceasing, contemplating, returning, and purity. These stages are called the "six wondrous teachings" or the "six mysterious doors" *(liu miao-fa men)* in Chinese. We will discuss them below.

1) *Counting the breath.* The first purpose of counting the breath is to relax the system and concentrate the mind. The second purpose is to focus the mind and engage it fully in the wonderful mystery of breathing. One should count the breath by counting either inhalations or exhalations, but not both. Counting is done in groups of ten. The breath should be allowed to flow freely without being forced in any way. After counting ten breaths, one should start over again. Thousands of years of experience with this technique have shown that if less than ten breaths are counted, the mind has a tendency to become hurried or impatient. If more than ten breaths are counted, the mind has a tendency to become unfocused and scattered. Experience has also shown that there are three basic problems that often crop up when people practice this technique: a) people count only eight or nine breaths

when they have actually breathed ten times; b) people count eleven or twelve breaths when they have actually breathed only ten times; c) people confuse inhalation with exhalation. The best way to avoid these problems is to concentrate and be very mindful of what you are doing. This is one time when it is very important to practice precise concentration on the task at hand.

Our mental attitude is always very important. When we meditate, our attitude reverberates within itself and creates its own storms or its own expanses of peace and wisdom. When counting the breath, it is important to avoid the two extremes of being overly anxious or overly relaxed. If we are too anxious, our bodies become tense, and the energies in our systems do not flow properly. Similarly, if we allow ourselves to be too relaxed in our approach to this technique, our systems can become sleepy and dull.

The right way to approach breath-counting is to be sensitive to the interaction between the mind and the breath. If we calmly allow the mind and the breath to find their own interactive harmony, we discover that both the mind and the breath become very calm. Eventually, the mind seems to breathe on its own, without use of the lungs.

2) *Mentally following the breath.* After a while, a beautiful harmony between mind and breath becomes established, and it is no longer necessary to count inhalations or exhalations. This point can be identified by the peace and calm that begins to permeate the system, and by the ease with which the mind willingly follows each breath through its full course of entering the nose and the lungs and then leaving again. When this stage is reached, one need only observe or follow the flow of the breath. One

should be able to do this almost without effort.

3) *Ceasing.* After the mind has followed the breath for some time and a peaceful harmony has been established between mind and breath, the mind becomes exceptionally calm. This slows the breath even further and leads the entire system into a state of wonderful ceasing. At this point, true contemplation can begin.

4) *Contemplation.* At this point, the time is right to contemplate the breath in the light of all of the mind's wisdom. Contemplate that the breath depends on the body, and the body depends on the breath. Contemplate that the body is comprised of nothing more than the six forms of sense awareness (eye, ear, nose, tongue, body, and mind) and that the personality is comprised of nothing more than the five skandhas (form, sensation, perception, mental activity, and consciousness). This contemplation is very effective in breaking the hold of self-grasping and attachment to the things of this world.

5) *Returning.* Turn the mind in on itself; return its radiance wholly to itself. Contemplate this returning and see that all mental phenomena are illusions and that all that the mind grasps is an illusion. Only the deepest lights of the mind are real. As its delusions are seen through more and more, the mind will discover that it basks in perfect wisdom without outflows and that it has always basked in this wisdom.

6) *Purity.* When the mind no longer grasps at anything, it becomes pure. Like virtue, purity is its own reward, and like wisdom, purity knows itself. There are no words to describe this state.

If you gather your mind in samādhi,
you will understand the process
by which phenomena rise and fall.
—from the *Sūtra of Bequeathed Teachings*

CONCLUSION

The *Sūtra on the Contemplation of Mind* says:

> The mind is like a painter who is able to paint all things,
> and the mind is like a slave who is ordered about and
> controlled by suffering and trouble. The mind is like a
> king who is able to do whatever he wants, and the mind
> is like a stupid thief who brings ruination onto himself.

This passage amply describes the power of the mind—it
can be like a king or like a thief, like an artist or like a slave.
Through contemplation and meditation, we learn to use
our minds for their own benefit as we uncover their truly
boundless potential.

The five contemplations were designed to help each and
every one of us overcome specific problems in our practice
of Buddhism. Those who honestly decide to appraise themselves and then act on their appraisal with the sincere intention
of improving whatever they have found will discover that
these five contemplations are very powerful methods for
achieving positive growth and beneficial change. As with all
practical methods, the five contemplations must be practiced consistently over a long enough period of time to be
fully effective.

In using them, it is important to remember that, once we
have overcome a particular problem, we should change the

remedy we are using. For example, if we have made progress in curing greed by using the contemplation on uncleanness, then it is time to begin using the contemplation on compassion. If one overuses the contemplation on uncleanness, one may develop an unhealthy revulsion toward life in this world. That is not the purpose of this contemplation. The purpose of the contemplation on uncleanness is only to overcome greed and attachment and nothing more.

Śākyamuni Buddha praised wisdom above all of the other virtues. In a sense, all the virtues are nothing but facets of wisdom. In our practice of Buddhism, each one of us must develop wisdom. First we stop, then we think, then we decide. By doing this many times, we gradually become wise. The five contemplations are methods to help us in this process of growth. Their benefits are there waiting for all who want them.

GLOSSARY

Āgamas. (*Skt.* source of the teaching) A collection of very early Buddhist writings in the Sanskrit canon. Early and basic teachings of the Buddha. They are essentially the same as the Pāli Nikāyas.

ālaya consciousness. (*Skt. ālaya-vijñāna.* storehouse consciousness) Often called the eighth consciousness or the container consciousness. It is the level of consciousness in which all karmic seeds are stored.

Amitābha Buddha. (*Skt.* boundless light) The buddha of mercy and wisdom. Amitābha is one of the most popular buddhas in Mahāyāna Buddhism. He presides over the western pure land.

anāpāna. (*Skt.* inhalation-exhalation) A basic technique of counting the breath for the purpose of achieving mental concentration.

anuttara-samyak-sambodhi. (*Skt.* unexcelled complete enlightenment) Complete, unexcelled enlightenment— an attribute of all buddhas.

bodhi. (*Skt.* enlightenment) Enlightened. Awakened to one's own buddha nature.

bodhi mind. (*Skt. bodhicitta.* enlightenment mind) The enlightened mind or the mind that seeks enlightenment. The precise definition is, the inspiration to achieve complete enlightenment on behalf of all sentient beings.

bodhi way. (*Skt. bodhi.* enlightenment) The way to enlightenment. The path of a Buddhist who is actively seeking enlightenment.

bodhisattva. (*Skt.* enlightened being) 1) Any person who is seeking buddhahood. 2) A highly realized being who stands right on the edge of nirvāṇa but remains in this world to help others achieve enlightenment.

buddha. (*Skt.* awakened one) There are innumerable buddhas in the universe. Śākyamuni Buddha was the historical buddha who taught the Dharma on earth. He is generally thought to have lived during the years 463–383 BC.

ch'an. *See* zen.

Chih-i, Master. (538–597) Also known as the "Wise One," Chih-i was an important founder of T'ien-t'ai Buddhism.

conditioned arising. The Buddha's most basic insight into the workings of the phenomenal universe. Conditioned arising means that no thing and no phenomenon arises out of nothing and that no thing and no phenomenon can exist alone and by itself. Sometimes called dependent origination since all phenomena are dependent on each other.

desire realm. *See* three realms.

dhāraṇī. (*Skt.* holder) Incantations, including magical, symbolic, and sonically effective phrases.

Dharma. (*Skt.* carrying, holding) The teachings of the Buddha, which carry or hold the truth.

dharma. (*Skt.* thing) Dharma with a small "d" basically means anything that can be thought of or named. Often it is close in meaning to the English word phenomenon.

Dharmas can be mental events, the passage of time, the order in which things occur, and so on.

dharmadhātu. (*Skt.* dharma realm) The realm in which all dharmas arise and pass away.

dharmakāya. (*Skt.* body of the Dharma, body of the great order) The buddha nature that is identical with transcendent reality. The unity of the Buddha with everything that exists. One of the three buddha bodies (trikāya). The other two are the sambhogakāya and the nirmāṇakāya.

dhyāna. (*Skt.* absorption) Deep meditative adsorption or concentration.

eighteen realms. The six senses, plus the six sense organs, plus the six consciousnesses produced by these.

empty, emptiness. *(Skt. śūnyatā)* Having no essence or permanent aspect whatsoever. All phenomena are empty. Sometimes translated as "transparent" or "open."

five precepts. The five basic moral precepts of Buddhism: no killing, no stealing, no lying, no sexual misconduct, no use of drugs or alcohol.

five skandhas. (*Skt.* heap) The five basic "heaps" of psychophysical parts that are the building blocks of a person. They are form, sensation, perception, mental activity, and consciousness.

form realm. *See* three realms.

formless realm. *See* three realms.

Hīnayāna. (*Skt.* small vehicle) Not to be confused with modern Theravāda Buddhism. The word Hīnayāna is

used in Chinese to denote self-centered Buddhist practices that are not concerned with the well-being of others.

Hua-yen School. One of China's eight major schools of
Buddhism. The Hua-yen School, which emphasizes the
interconnectedness of all things, is based on the teachings
of the *Avataṃsaka Sūtra.*

Hui-neng, Master. (638–713) A very influential Zen master, Hui-neng was the sixth patriarch of the Chinese Zen
lineage.

karma. (*Skt.* work, action) The universal law of cause and
effect concerned with intentional deeds. All intentional
deeds produce effects that eventually will be felt by the
doer of the deed. Good deeds produce good karmic effects
while bad deeds produce bad karmic effects. Good deeds
are deeds that help sentient beings while bad deeds are
deeds that harm them.

Kuei-feng, Master. (780–841) Also known as Tsung-mi.
The fifth patriarch of the Hua-yen School of Chinese
Buddhism.

Mahāyāna. (*Skt.* great vehicle) One of the two great branches of Buddhism (Theravāda is the other one). Mahāyāna
Buddhism stresses compassion above asceticism.

mudrā. (*Skt.*) A gesture or position of the hands, especially
when meditating.

nidāna. *(Pāli) See* twelve causal conditions.

nirmāṇakāya. (*Skt.* transformation body) The body of a
buddha as he appears to most people. One of the three
buddha bodies (trikāya). The other two are the sambhogakāya and the dharmakāya. A buddha's nirmāṇakāya is a

compassionate projection of his sambhogakāya.

nirvāṇa. (*Skt.* extinction) Extinction of all causes leading to rebirth. The ultimate goal of all Buddhist practice. Nirvāṇa is not complete annihilation, but rather another mode of existence.

outflow. *(Skt. asrava)* Any mental defilement that creates karma.

pāramitā. *See* six pāramitās.

parinirvāṇa. (*Skt.* total nirvāṇa) The great nirvāṇa of Śākyamuni Buddha. His death.

prajñā. (*Skt.* wisdom) The highest form of wisdom. The highest of the six pāramitās.

prātimokṣa. (*Skt.* deliverance) The rules that govern the lives of Buddhist monks and nuns.

precepts. *See* five precepts.

Pure Land School. Based on the *Amitābha Sūtra,* Pure Land Buddhism is the most popular form of Buddhism in East Asia. In Pure Land Buddhism, emphasis is placed on the power of Amitābha Buddha to help the practitioner. One of China's eight major schools of Buddhism.

Śākyamuni Buddha. The founder of Buddhism. *See* buddha.

samādhi. (*Skt.* to concentrate) A profound state of meditative equipoise.

sambhogakāya. (*Skt.* reward body, body of delight) The body in which a buddha experiences the joy of his enlightenment. One of the three buddha bodies (trikāya). The other two are the dharmakāya and the nirmāṇakāya.

Images of Amitābha Buddha in Buddhist art are often representations of his sambhogakāya.

saṃsāra. (*Skt.* journeying) Delusion. Deluded mental activity that keeps the mind trapped in the cycle of birth and death.

saṅgha. (*Skt.* crowd) The Buddhist community. All followers of Buddhism. The Chinese term for saṅgha usually refers only to Buddhist monks and nuns.

sarvajñā. (*Skt.* omniscience) The omniscience, wisdom, and perfect knowledge of a buddha.

śāstra. (*Skt.* instructions) Philosophical and didactic commentaries written on Buddhist sutras by Mahāyāna thinkers.

śīla. (*Skt.* precepts, obligations) Basic morality.

Single Vehicle. The "one path" that contains the essence of all of the Buddha's teachings. The *Lotus Sūtra* is a Single Vehicle teaching.

six guidelines. *(Skt. saddharma)*

six pāramitās. (*Skt. pāramitā.* that which has reached the other shore) The transcendental truths, sometimes called perfections, that inform and guide Buddhist practice. They are: generosity, upholding the precepts, patience, energetic progress, meditation, and wisdom.

six realms. The six realms of existence are hell, hungry ghost, animal, human, asura, and heaven.

six senses. The six senses are: sight, smell, hearing, taste, touch, and the thinking processes that coordinate these.

skandha. *See* five skandhas.

śrāvaka. (*Skt.* one who heard) Any one of the Buddha's personal disciples.

sūtra. (*Skt.* threads) That which is "threaded together," the sacred scriptures of Buddhism.

T'an-luan, Master. (476–sometime after 545) An early Pure Land master.

T'ang Dynasty. (618–906) Until the imperial suppression of Buddhism in 845, the T'ang Dynasty was China's greatest period of Buddhism.

Tao–an, Master. (312–385) One of China's first and greatest monks. Tao-an is especially remembered for his ability to speak about the Dharma and draw people to it.

Tao-hsuan, Master. (596–667) An important early master within the Vinaya School of Chinese Buddhism.

tathāgata. (*Skt.* thus gone one) One of the ten names of the Buddha.

three realms. *(Skt. triloka)* Three different realms that make up saṃsāra. The three realms are the desire realm (kāmadhātu), the form realm (rūpadhātu) and the formless realm (arūpadhātu). The cycle of the existence of all beings in the six realms takes place within the three realms.

T'ien-t'ai School. One of China's eight major schools of Buddhism. The T'ien-t'ai School emphasizes balancing practice and study.

Tsung-mi, Master. (780–841) *See* Kuei-feng, Master.

Tu-hsun, Master. (557–640) The first patriarch of the Hua-yen School in China.

twelve causal conditions. In Sanskrit they are called the twelve nidānas. Sometimes called the twelve links. The twelve basic links that make up the chain of deluded existence. They are: ignorance, activity, awareness, name and form, the six senses (eye, ear, nose, tongue, body, mind), contact, sensation, desire, grasping, being, birth, and death.

twelve dimensions. The six senses (eye, ear, nose, tongue, body, and the thinking processes that coordinate these) plus the six realms (form, sound, smell, taste, touch, mental dharmas).

udumbara flower. *ficus glomerata.* A rare and beautiful flower. In Buddhist sūtras it is used as a metaphor for the rare appearance of a buddha on earth.

Vairocana Buddha. (*Skt. Vairocana.* he who is like the sun) The personification of the dharmakāya, Vairocana Buddha is especially important in esoteric Buddhism.

zen. (*Skt. dhyāna, Chinese ch'an)* Japanese pronunciation of the Chinese transliteration of the Sanskrit word "dhyāna," which means "meditation" or "absorption." The school of Zen Buddhism is one of the eight major schools of Chinese Buddhism.

TABLE OF CHINESE TERMS

TECHNICAL TERMS

ālaya consciousness
阿賴耶識

anāpāna
安那般那

aniyata
不定、不定法

anuttara-samyak-sambodhi
阿耨多羅三藐三菩提

argumentative anger
諍論瞋

auspicious position
吉祥坐

being able to take it
能安忍

bodhi
菩提

bodhi mind
菩提心

bodhisattva
菩提薩埵、菩薩

breaking the hold of all phenomena
破法遍

buddha
佛陀

ceasing and contemplating with skillful tranquility
善巧安心止觀

ch'an
禪

chih
止

chih-kuan
止觀

complete and sudden
圓頓止觀

conditioned arising
緣起

consciousness without boundaries
識無邊處定

contemplation going against the flow
of the many-varied causal conditions
雜染逆觀

contemplation going with the flow
of the many-varied causal conditions
雜染順觀

contemplation of doubt
觀疑

contemplation of the indescribable realm
觀不思議境

contemplation of knowing where you really are
知次住

contemplation of the thirty-seven conditions
leading to buddhahood
道品調適

contemplation on a moment of thought
and the twelve causal conditions
一念十二因緣

contemplation on breathing
數息觀

contemplation on Buddha
念佛觀

contemplation on compassion
慈悲觀

contemplation on conditioned arising
緣起觀

contemplation on karmic fruits
and the twelve causal conditions
觀果報十二因緣

contemplation on the importance
of arousing the bodhi mind
發真正菩提心

contemplation on uncleanness
不淨觀

demon-subduing position
降魔坐

desire realm
欲界

dhāraṇī
陀羅尼

Dharma
法

dharmadhātu
法界

dharmakāya
法身

dhyāna
禪那

dhyāna heaven
禪天

dhyāna of not thinking and not not thinking
非想非非想處定

door of arising and non-arising
生即無生門

door of contemplating
觀察門

door of ending both contemplation and language
語觀雙絕門

door of observing phenomena
to overcome belief in the self
法有我無門

door of uniting basis and form
事理圓融門

door of vowing
作願門

duṣkṛta
突吉羅

eight dhyānas
八定

eighteen realms
十八界

emptiness
空

emptiness without boundaries
空無邊處定

examining
伺

five contemplations
五停心觀

five skandhas
五蘊

form realm
色界

formless realm
無色界

four ch'an
四禪

four kinds of samādhi
四種三昧

four necessary principles
法四依

great universal samādhi
方等三昧

greatest joy of this world
世間第一樂事

half-walking half-sitting samādhi
半行半坐三昧

hsi (attach)
繫

hua t'ou
話頭

Hua-yen samādhi
華嚴三昧

karma
業

kuan
觀

long-sitting samādhi
常坐三昧

long-walking samādhi
常行三昧

method of the directed cure
對治助開

mudrā
手印

nirmāṇakāya
應身、應化身

nirvāṇa
涅槃

non-localized dhyāna
無所有處定

not-sitting not-walking samādhi
非行非坐三昧

ocean of breath
氣海

one mind-two doors
一心二門

outflow
漏

pārājika
波羅夷

pāramitā
波羅蜜多

parinirvāṇa
般涅槃

pāyattika
波逸提

perfect equanimity
離法愛

prajñā
般若

pratideśanīya
波羅提提捨尼

prātimokṣa
波羅提木叉

pure contemplation going against the flow
of the many-varied causal conditions
清淨逆觀

pure contemplation going with the flow
of the many-varied causal conditions
清淨順觀

reasonable anger
順理瞋

samādhi
定、禪定、三摩地、三昧、止

śamatha
舍摩他

sambhogakāya
報身

saṃsāra
輪迴

saṅgaveṣa
僧殘

saṅgha
僧伽

sapta adhikaraṇa śamathāḥ
七滅諍法

sarvajñā
一切智

searching
尋

seven pure flowers
七淨華

seven purities
七淨、七種淨德

she (detachment)
捨

śikṣamāna
式叉摩那

śīla
尸羅

six consciousnesses
六識

six guidelines
六法

six pāramitās
六波羅蜜多

six senses
六識

sixteen exceptional dharmas
十六特勝法

skandha
蘊

śrāmaṇeraka
沙彌

śramaṇerikā
沙彌尼

śrāvaka
聲聞

śūraṅgama
首楞嚴

tathāgata
如來

ten vehicles of contemplation
十乘觀法

three realms
三界

three trainings
三學

twelve causal conditions (nidānas)
十二因緣

twelve dimensions
十二入

udumbara flower
優曇跋羅華

upāsaka
優婆塞

upāsikā
優婆夷

understanding loss and gain
知得失

unreasonable anger
違理瞋

Vinaya
毗奈耶、律

vipaśyanā
毗婆舍那

vision of the buddhas samādhi
佛立三昧

PROPER NAMES

Amitābha
阿彌陀佛

Chih-i, Master
智顗大師

Hīnayāna
小乘

Hua-yen School
華嚴宗

Hui-neng, Master
慧能大師

Kuei-feng, Master
圭峰大師

Mahāyāna
大乘

Mañjughoṣa
妙音

Mañjuśrī
文殊師利

Mind-Only School
唯識宗

Pure Land School
淨土宗

Śākyamuni
釋迦牟尼佛

Śāriputra
舍利弗

Single Vehicle
一乘

Subhūti
須菩提

T'an-luan, Master
曇鸞大師

T'ang Dynasty
唐朝

Tao–an, Master
道安大師

Tao-hsuan, Master
道宣大師

Theravāda
上座部

T'ien-t'ai School
天台宗

Tsung-mi, Master
宗密大師

Tu-hsun, Master
杜順大師

Vairocana
毗盧遮那佛

Wa-kuan Temple
瓦官寺

Yogācāra
瑜伽宗、法相宗

SŪTRAS AND COMMENTARIES

Abhidharma-skandha-pāda Śāstra
阿毘達磨法蘊足論

Abhidharmakośa
阿毘達磨俱舍論

Āgamas
阿含經

Avataṃsaka Sūtra
大方廣佛華嚴經

Awakening of Faith in the Mahāyāna
大乘起信論

Collection of Terms Used in Translation
翻譯名義集

Eight Realizations of the Bodhisattva Sūtra
八大人覺經

Five Part Vinaya
五分律

Four Part Vinaya
四分律

Graduated Explication of the Perfection of Meditation
釋禪波羅蜜次第法門

Great Treatise on the Perfection of Wisdom
大智度論

Great Universal Dhāraṇī Sūtra
大方廣陀羅尼經

Lotus Sūtra
妙法蓮華經

Madhyamāgama
中阿含經

Mahāparinirvāṇa Sūtra
大般涅槃經

Mahāprajñāpāramitā Sūtra
大般若經

Mahāsaṃnipāta Sūtra
大方等大集經

Mahāyānābhidharma-samuccaya-vyākhyā Śāstra
大乘阿毘達磨雜集論

Mañjughoṣa chapter of the Lotus Sūtra
妙法蓮華經妙音菩薩品

Mañjuśrī-paripṛccha Sūtra
文殊菩薩問經

Mūlasarvāstivāda-vinaya-kṣudrakavastu
根本說一切有部毗奈耶

Pratyutpanna-buddha-sammukhāvasthitā-samādhi Sūtra
般舟三昧經、十方現在佛悉在前立定經

Pravara-deva-rāja-paripṛccha Sūtra
勝天王般若波羅蜜經

Revision of the Four Part Vinaya
四分律珊繁補闕行事鈔

Saṃyuktāgama
雜阿含經

Six Wondrous Teachings
六妙門

Śubhavyūha-rāja chapter of the Lotus Sūtra
妙法蓮華經妙莊嚴王本事品

Sukhāvatīvyūha Sūtra
無量壽經

Śūraṅgama Sūtra
大佛頂首楞嚴經

Sūtra of Bequeathed Teachings
佛遺教經

Sūtra of Mañjuśrī's Discourse on Prajñā Wisdom
文殊說般若經

Sūtra of the Bodhisattva Stages
菩薩地持經

Sūtra on the Contemplation of Mind
心地觀經

Treatise on the Completion of Truth
成實論

Treatise on the Resources of the Bodhi Way
菩提資糧論

Treatise on the Sūtra of Discrimination
分別經論

Twelve Names of the Buddha Sūtra
十二佛名經

Vimalakīrtinirdeśa Sūtra
維摩詰所說經

Vinaya in Ten Recitations
十誦律

Yogācārabhūmi Śāstra
瑜伽師地論

INDEX

ABOUT THE CONTRIBUTORS

JOHN R. MCRAE received his Ph.D. from Yale University in 1983 and is professor of East Asian Buddhism at Indiana University in Bloomington. His earliest research was on the earliest period of Chinese Ch'an, or Zen, Buddhism, published as *The Northern School and the Formation of Early Ch'an Buddhism* (University of Hawaii Press, 1986). The companion volume has been in the works for a long time and is tentatively titled: *Evangelical Zen: Shen-hui (684–758), Sudden Enlightenment, and the Southern School of Chinese Ch'an Buddhism*. Recently, he initiated a long-term cooperative study of esoteric Buddhism and popular religion in Yunnan in southwest China based on previously unpublished handwritten manuscripts, art historical materials, and ethnographic data.

TOM GRAHAM has been doing Chinese studies for over twenty-five years, ten of which he spent living in East Asia. He has translated for numerous publications, including another recent book by Master Hsing Yun entitled *Being Good: Buddhist Ethics for Everyday Life* (Weatherhill, 1998). He lives in San Diego, California.

ABOUT FO GUANG SHAN

THE FO GUANG SHAN BUDDHIST ORDER and its affiliated temples and educational institutions in the International Buddhist Progress Society (IBPS) and the Buddha's Light International Association (BLIA) were founded by Master Hsing Yun and follow his nonsectarian teachings of Humanistic Buddhism. The United States headquarters for Master Hsing Yun's activities are at Hsi Lai Temple near Los Angeles.

Humanistic Buddhism affirms that the Buddha was born in this human world, cultivated himself in this human world, was enlightened in this human world, and taught beings the way to experience nirvāṇa in this human world and not apart from it. Humanistic Buddhism teaches that we can live in the world fully and practice Buddhism at the same time. Humanistic Buddhism encourages us to integrate the Buddha's teachings of tolerance, loving-kindness, compassion, joyfulness, and equanimity into our lives for our benefit and for the benefit of all beings.

To learn more about Humanistic Buddhism and the activities of Master Hsing Yun, please contact:

Hsi Lai Temple
3456 South Glenmark Drive
Hacienda Heights CA 91745 USA
Phone: (626) 961-9697
Fax: (626) 369-1944
www.hsilai.org
info@hsilai.org

ABOUT WISDOM

Wisdom Publications, a not-for-profit publisher, is dedicated to making available authentic Buddhist works for the benefit of all. We publish translations of the sutras and tantras, commentaries and teachings of past and contemporary Buddhist masters, and original works by the world's leading Buddhist scholars. We publish our titles with the appreciation of Buddhism as a living philosophy and with the special commitment to preserve and transmit important works from all the major Buddhist traditions.

If you would like more information or a copy of our mail-order catalog, please contact us at:

Wisdom Publications
199 Elm Street
Somerville, Massachusetts 02144 USA
Telephone: (617) 776-7416
Fax: (617) 776-7841
Email: info@wisdompubs.org
Web Site: http://www.wisdompubs.org

The Wisdom Trust

As a not-for-profit publisher, Wisdom Publications is dedicated to the publication of fine Dharma books for the benefit of all sentient beings and dependent upon the kindness and generosity of sponsors in order to do so. If you would like to make a donation to Wisdom Publications, please do so through our Somerville office. If you would like to sponsor the publication of a book, please write or email us for more information.

Thank you.

Wisdom Publications is a non-profit, charitable 501(c)(3) organization and a part of the Foundation for the Preservation of the Mahayana Tradition (FPMT).